INDIA AND THE WORLD

Other Titles

Hindustan Times Leadership Initiative	*The Peace Dividend: Progress in India and South Asia*
Harinder Baweja (ed.)	*Most Wanted: Profiles of Terror*
Jawid Laiq	*The Maverick Republic*
J.N. Dixit (ed.)	*External Affairs: Cross-Border Relations*
M.J. Akbar	*India: The Siege Within*
M.J. Akbar	*Kashmir: Behind the Vale*
M.J. Akbar	*Nehru: The Making of India*
M.J. Akbar	*Riot after Riot*
M.J. Akbar	*The Shade of Swords*
M.J. Akbar	*By Line*
Meghnad Desai	*Nehru's Hero Dilip Kumar: In the Life of India*
Prafulla Roy, trans. John W. Hood	*In the Shadow of the Sun & Other Stories*
Rohan Gunaratna	*Inside Al Qaeda*
Rifaat Hussain, J.N. Dixit Julie Sirrs, Ajai Shukla Anand Giridharadas Rahimullah Yusufzai John Jennings	*Afghanistan and 9/11*
Satish Jacob	*From Hotel Palestine Baghdad*
Saad Bin Jung	*Wild Tales from the Wild*
Anil K. Jaggia and Saurabh Shukla	*IC 814: Hijacked! The Inside Story*
Eric S. Margolis	*War at the Top of the World*
Maj. Gen. Ian Cardozo	*Param Vir: Our Heroes in Battle*
Mushirul Hasan	*India Partitioned. 2 Vols*
Mushirul Hasan	*John Company to the Republic*
Mushirul Hasan	*Knowledge Power and Politics*
Rachel Dwyer	*Yash Chopra: Fifty Years of Indian Cinema*
Sujata S. Sabnis	*A Twist in Destiny*
Veena Sharma	*Kailash Mansarovar: A Sacred Journey*
V.N. Rai	*Curfew in the City*

Forthcoming Titles

V. Kurien	*Daring to Dream: An Autobiography*
Premchand, trans. Madan Gopal	*My Life and Times: An Autobiographical Narrative*
Duff Hart-Davis	*Honorary Tiger: The Life of Billy Arjan Singh*

EDITED BY

NAMITA BHANDARE

Lotus Collection

This edition published in 2005
The Lotus Collection
An imprint of
Roli Books Pvt Ltd
M-75, G.K. II Market
New Delhi 110 048
Phones: ++91 (011) 2921 2271, 2921 2782
2921 0886, Fax: ++91 (011) 2921 7185
E-mail: roli@vsnl.com; Website: rolibooks.com

Also at
Varanasi, Bangalore, Jaipur and the Netherlands

Cover : Arati Subramanyam
Layout: Narendra Shahi
Photo Credit: Hindustan Times

ISBN: 81-7436-401-3
Rs. 395

Typeset in Photina MT by Roli Books Pvt Ltd
Printed at Tan Prints (India) Pvt. Ltd., Jhajjar, Haryana

Contents

INDIA AND THE WORLD

A Blueprint for Partnership and Growth

Hindustan Times
Leadership Initiative

Dr Manmohan Singh
Prime Minister of India

Sonia Gandhi
Chairperson, United Progressive Alliance

Imran Khan
Founder, Tehreek-e-Insaf, Pakistan

Farooq Abdullah
Former Chief Minister, Jammu and Kashmir

P. Chidambaram
Union Minister for Finance

Arun Jaitley
Senior BJP Leader and Former Union Minister

Arun Shourie
Senior BJP Leader and Former Union Minister

Suresh Prabhakar Prabhu
Shiv Sena Leader and Former Union Minister

Chandrika Kumaratunga
President, Sri Lanka

John Major
Former Prime Minister, United Kingdom

Kiran Mazumdar-Shaw
Chairman and Managing Director, Biocon India

Mukesh D. Ambani

Chairman and Managing Director, Reliance Industries Ltd

Nandan M. Nilekani

CEO, President and Managing Director, Infosys Technologies

Subir Raha

Chairman and Managing Director, Oil & Natural Gas Corporation Ltd

Dr Hans Blix

Former Head, UN Monitoring Verification and Inspection Commission for Iraq

Dr Surakiart Sathirathai

Minister of Foreign Affairs of Thailand

K. Natwar Singh

Minister of External Affairs of India

Altaf Hussain
Founder, Muttahida Quami Movement, Pakistan

Dr Henry Kissinger
Former Secretary of State, United States of America

Shobhana Bhartia
Vice-chairperson, Hindustan Times

INDIA AND THE WORLD

A Blueprint for Partnership and Growth

Hindustan Times

Leadership Initiative

A serious newspaper must go beyond reporting the news of the day. It must contribute to intellectual debate, find solutions to problems that vex civil society and set the agenda for a better future.

It is with this belief that the country's most respected newspaper, *Hindustan Times* launched its Leadership Initiative series in 2003. Every year, the media group brings together key political and business leaders, strategists and thinkers from India and the world.

Over two days of intensive discussion, the Leadership Initiative, 2004, played host to such figures as the Prime Minister of India Dr Manmohan Singh, United Progressive Alliance Chairperson Sonia Gandhi, former British Prime Minister John Major, President of Sri Lanka Chandrika Bandaranaike Kumaratunga and Nobel Laureate and former US Secretary of State Dr Henry Kissinger.

On the agenda was a variety of topics that touched on the paradigms of the changing world and the possible role South Asia and India could play.

After two days of intensive discussions and interactions, the Leadership Initiative was able to throw up many solutions but more important, pose several questions. It was, in the words of Sonia Gandhi, 'An occasion for many of us to step back from the preoccupations of our daily lives and reflect on larger and more crucial issues.'

> There can be no greater example of democracy's success than in India. Nowhere in the world do so many people of such variety and of such disparate incomes practice their franchise successfully and peacefully and repeatedly.

Welcome
Address

▪

Shobhana Bhartia
Vice-chairperson, Hindustan Times

▪

THE LEADERSHIP INITIATIVE REPRESENTS OUR EFFORT TO CONTRIBUTE TO THE DEBATE ON IMPORTANT ISSUES THAT AFFECT INDIA AND THE world. We believe that a serious newspaper such as the *Hindustan Times* needs to do more than just report the news of the day. It needs to be at the forefront of intellectual debate in the country where it is read and the world in which it exists.

Through the leadership initiative the *Hindustan Times* aims to provide a creative hand in shaping the future and in giving voice to the concerns of the present. We aim to provide an annual platform where some of the most insightful minds of the generation share their ideas, experiences and solutions to some of the problems that still bedevil this region and the world.

Last year, the leadership initiative looked at the prospects for peace and prosperity in South Asia. We were still reeling under the shock of a post 9/11 world. In Washington and in London, in Delhi and in Islamabad, in Kabul and in Baghdad, the ramifications of the collapse of the twin towers of the World Trade Center were still being felt. There was a growing recognition that the world had ignored conflicts in isolated regions at its own peril.

The Peace Dividend, the theme of last year's leadership initiative reflected that sense of urgency and we were gratified that soon after our conference the then Prime Minister Mr Atal Behari Vajpayee resumed a peace process with Pakistan that has lost none of its momentum under his successor Dr Manmohan Singh. We can hardly claim credit but in some small way we like to think that we were there when it all began.

If the mood last year was one of closure – the imperative need to resolve conflicts – the mood this year strikes me as being more forward-looking; towards ushering economic prosperity, the fruits of which can be shared by every citizen on our planet.

Peace and prosperity are fundamentally interlinked. Peace

is not just the absence of war but a precondition to economic progress. Conversely, the lack of economic progress can lead to instability and frustration that have the potential to shake the very foundations of international order. If there is a positive outcome of the horrific events of 9/11 it is this: it has taught us the value of pooling our strengths together to combat terrorism. It has shown us the way forward in working together for the betterment of humanity.

In this conference, we will share the insights of world leaders on the paradigms of the changing world and the possible role South Asia and India, in particular, can play.

The challenges that confront a globalised world are more complex and intense. Economic integration also makes for shared vulnerability. A single virus can knock out complex computer systems and a bombed pipeline can slow down the wheels of commerce. Hostage-takers whether in Beslan or Baghdad and regardless of whether the hostages are innocent schoolchildren or truck drivers from Punjab still have the frightening power to undermine everything that the world has been working towards. With the forces of fundamentalist terrorism stalking the globe, the world needs to combat serious threats that might be even greater.

We know also that India is becoming a global player in a whole range of services and technological fields. Indian firms have made a name for themselves around the world in not only information technology but also in pharmaceuticals, biotechnology, finance and telecommunications. India is also slowly establishing a foothold in manufacturing in overseas markets. The principal challenge is, of course, poverty and underdevelopment but it requires no great insight to say that the answers to these problems can only be located within the structure of a rapidly growing economy.

We grew at about 6 per cent in the last decade but there is need to step it up to 8 per cent or even 10 per cent in the years to come. We have also learned that this economic growth is meaningless if it does not serve the needs of those who continue to live below the poverty line or touch the lives of rural India where 65 per cent of our people reside.

Dr Manmohan Singh has shown us that the idea of reforms with a human face is not just an empty slogan. People at the lowest rung of the social and economic ladder must be empowered through the advancement of education, better healthcare, and employment opportunities so that they too are partners in the creation of a vibrant new India.

But the challenges we must face are not restricted to just within our borders. What do Indian business leaders feel about competing in a global economy? We will also consider if India can ever hope to become the next economic superpower and what are the triggers that will set this off.

Our canvas goes beyond India. We have with us some of the brightest minds of South Asia to talk to us about regional cooperation for growth and peace. How can we keep South Asia together? Can we identify the issues that unite us? Is there a specific South Asian identity amidst all our diversity and how best can we use this to our advantage in a global environment? Finally we need to look afresh at India and Pakistan not just in terms of a historically troubled relationship but in new areas of peace and prosperity.

India has been at the forefront of a sometimes very lonely battle against terrorism. Well before current concerns about nuclear proliferation reached today's levels, India was warning the world about the spread of weapons of mass destruction and well before the world today began debating whether democracy is a true antidote to terrorism India was applying this political balm to extremism at home.

Democracy and consensus are essential prerequisites to the blueprint that we are seeking to create. There can be no greater example of democracy's success than in India. Nowhere in the world do so many people of such variety and of such disparate incomes practice their franchise successfully and peacefully and repeatedly.

Some of the leading minds from very disparate political ideologies and streams of thought will present their views on democracy and India in the twenty-first century. During the course of the conference, we will have the privilege of listening to leaders in public life from within India, within the region and within the world discuss these three themes – economy, security and democracy – that form the matrix through which the concerns of the world today can be best understood. We will question them and discuss issues with them. At the end of the conference, I trust we will have come up with some answers on how best to map the blueprint for partnership and growth.

India and the world are not boats floating apart. They are ships that sail in tandem. India is more confident, India is more global and, as a consequence, the world is a little more Indian.

We seek mutually beneficial relations with all our Asian neighbours and will work closely with Asia to realise our combined aspiration to make the twenty-first century an Asian century. We want a neighbourhood of peace and shared prosperity in which people, goods and services can travel with ease across borders.

Inaugural **Address**

Dr Manmohan Singh

Dr Manmohan Singh

Prime Minister of India

The fourteenth Prime Minister of India, Dr Manmohan Singh is highly regarded for both his diligence and academic approach to work as well as his accessibility and unassuming demeanour.

Prime Minister Manmohan Singh was born on 26 September 1932 in a village in the Punjab province of undivided India. He earned a first class honours degree in economics in 1957 from the University of Cambridge. Dr Singh followed this with a DPhil in economics from Nuffield College at Oxford University in 1962.

Dr Singh's academic credentials were burnished by the years he spent teaching at Punjab University and the prestigious Delhi School of Economics. He subsequently served as Secretary General of the South Commission in Geneva.

The many governmental positions that Dr Singh has held include, Secretary in the Ministry of Finance; Deputy Chairman of the Planning Commission; Governor of the Reserve Bank of India; Advisor to the Prime Minister; and, Chairman of the University Grants Commission.

Dr Singh spent five years between 1991 and 1996 as India's Finance Minister, a period that was the turning point in the economic history of independent India. His role in ushering in a comprehensive policy of economic reforms is now recognised worldwide.

Among the many awards and honours conferred upon Dr Singh, the most prominent, are India's second highest civilian honour, the Padma Vibhushan (1987). He also received the Asia Money Award for Finance Minister of the Year (1993 and 1994) and the Euro Money Award for Finance Minister of the Year (1993). Dr Singh has also been honoured by a number of other associations including by the Japanese Nihon Keizai Shimbun.

In his political career, Dr Singh has been a member of India's Upper House of Parliament, the Rajya Sabha, since 1991, where he was Leader of the Opposition between 1998 and 2004.

Dr Singh and his wife Mrs Gursharan Kaur have three daughters.

I AM DELIGHTED TO BE HERE IN YOUR MIDST TO INAUGURATE THE *HINDUSTAN TIMES* LEADERSHIP INITIATIVE CONFERENCE ON THE THEME *INDIA AND THE WORLD: A Blueprint for Partnership and Growth.*

The conference has by now become an important annual feature in the intellectual calendar of our national capital. I do wish I had the time to be here right through your deliberations so as to learn from the wealth of intellectual opinion gathered here.

The theme of *India and the World* has often been debated in this country over the past half century. From the time of our independence, when we tried to refashion our interaction with the outside world, this has been a subject of considerable discussion. The intellectual foundation for this debate was laid by Mahatma Gandhi when he said, 'I want the winds from every corner to blow through my house, but I refuse to be swept off my feet by any of them.'

Pandit Jawaharlal Nehru echoed this idea, while emphasising the importance of national sovereignty in shaping the interaction with the outside world, when he wrote in the *Discovery of India,* 'Today India swings between a blind adherence to her old customs and slavish imitation of foreign ways. In neither of these can she find relief or life or growth. India will find herself again when freedom opens out new horizons, and the future will then fascinate her far more than the immediate past of frustration and humiliation.' Panditji hoped that with freedom gained India, 'Will go forward with confidence, rooted in herself and yet eager to learn from others and cooperate with them. It is obvious that she has to come out of her shell and take full part in the life and activities of the modern age.'

To 'take full part in the life and activities of the modern age' and to establish 'partnerships for growth' are, indeed, the challenges that we have been grappling with in our interactions with the world. Perhaps no other post-colonial nation has debated so intensely and in so open a manner the terms of engagement with the world as we have in India. In the early years of decolonisation, later through the heat of the Cold War and, more recently, through the rough and tumble of the post-Cold War era we have debated at length the nature of our relationship with the world, the possibilities of partnership and the potential for growth. Broadly speaking the debate has been within two perspectives: the political and strategic and the economic and commercial.

When you title your conference theme as *India and the World: A Blueprint for Partnership and Growth*, I believe you are looking at political and economic partnerships and would like to see how these will accelerate the process of economic growth.

Undoubtedly, these issues lie at the core of our concerns. Our foreign policy and our economic policy have evolved over the years to enable us to derive the benefits of our interaction with the world while addressing the challenges that have come our way. While there are bound to be political differences in priorities and perceptions in a democracy, it must be recognised that there has been a great element of continuity, mirroring an evolving consensus, on many aspects of our foreign and external economic policy. I draw your attention to the fact that the initial response of our government in the early 1990s to the new post-Cold War world has since evolved, under successive governments, in a direction set by us at that time. Be it our foreign policy, both with respect to major powers and other nations, or our external economic policy, there has been continuity with change. I am sure the conference will devote time to a deeper consideration of these issues. Suffice it for me to say that in the heat and dust of our domestic debates on foreign and external economic policy we should not lose sight of the fact of this emerging consensus on our political and economic interaction with the outside world.

I sincerely believe that India's standing in the world will, in the final analysis, be defined by our domestic capabilities, by the well-being and creativity of our people, by the resilience of our political and social institutions.

Our government would like to give highest priority to an acceleration of the rate of economic growth through a process of economic and social development that is equitable and just. As an open society and an open economy we will have to engage the world at all levels and in all spheres. It is with this understanding that we seek a larger role for ourselves in global institutions and would like to help strengthen broad base multilateral institutions. India has to be an active trading nation and is, therefore, committed to strengthening a rule-based, transparent, non-discriminatory and consensual multilateral trading regime.

India's economic engagement with the world must match up to our size and scope. I would like to see closer and wider economic engagement between India and our Asian neighbourhood. I would like our business leaders to explore the full potential of the creation of an Asian economic community. We seek mutually beneficial relations with all our neighbours and will work closely with them to realise our combined aspiration to make the twenty-first century an Asian century. We would like to see a widening and deepening of our economic relations with China, Japan, the member countries of the Association of Southeast Asia Nations (ASEAN), the Central Asian Republics and our traditional friends in West Asia and Africa. We want a neighbourhood of peace and shared prosperity in which people, goods and services can travel with ease across borders.

South Asia must regain its pre-eminence in the global economy as a subcontinent of great creativity and enterprise. We would like to inject new energy into regional associations like the South Asian Association for Regional Cooperation (SAARC) and the Bay of Bengal Initiative for Multi-Sectoral, Technical and Economic Cooperation (BIMSTEC). It is in our shared interest to wage a giant struggle against poverty and ignorance.

We will continue to strengthen our wide-ranging and many-sided relationship with the United States, European Union and Russia. As a responsible nuclear power we are firmly committed to nuclear non-proliferation and will cooperate with the world community to prevent the proliferation of weapons of mass destruction and deal with the threat of terrorism. India is committed to work with the international community to make the world a safer place to live in.

We will pursue energy security within a cooperative framework working with other countries to ensure the security of oil supplies, of pipelines and sea-lanes of communication. We are equally committed to working with the international community in tackling other global threats. The threats to the environment, the threat of communicable diseases and the pandemic of HIV/AIDS are all global challenges. The world is a 'global village' and so we must address these challenges as members of a cooperative global community.

An important aspect of our interaction with the world is the role of the so-called Indian 'diaspora'. There is a strong emotional link between the global community of people of Indian origin and the Motherland. I am convinced that if we create at home the right environment and the required infrastructure we can draw on the tremendous creativity and enterprise of overseas Indians in building a more vibrant and dynamic economy at home.

I would like to take this opportunity to focus your attention on an altogether different aspect of our interaction with the world. This pertains to a dialogue between nations and civilisations. An ancient, civilisational nation like ours, home to more than one great religion of the world and many philosophical traditions; a land of linguistic and cultural diversity; and located at Asia's cultural crossroads, has quite naturally and understandably a unique position in the world. The world expects us to bring to the table of global discourse something more than strategic partnerships and market opportunities, important as both these are and open as we are to engaging the world on both these fronts.

I submit to you that India has something more to offer, that is specially relevant to the ongoing global discourse pertaining to the two great challenges of our time, namely, globalisation and the notion of a 'clash of civilisations'. Both these debates have often been conducted as if the debate is a battle between contending world-views. The media has often succumbed to the temptation of turning every dialogue into a debate by defining the terms of discussion in binary opposites. Are you 'for' or 'against'? Are you with 'us' or 'them'? Reality can never be captured in black and white. It is always represented in an array of colours.

India's unique contribution to the world has been the notion of the many-sidedness and the constant and continuing discovery of truth.

The idea of unity in diversity drawing on the wisdom of our forefathers who spoke of *Vasudhaiva kutumbakam* – which translates as 'the whole world is one family' – is a powerful yet practical political basis for dealing with these twin challenges of our times.

It is that philosophical tradition that inspired our freedom struggle and enabled a peaceful transfer of power in 1947. It is that notion of cooperative pluralism that was the basis of our democracy. Our democracy, like our civilisation, has been built on the notions of 'unity in diversity' and inclusive pluralism.

The idea of a 'clash of civilisations' goes against the grain of our civilisation. Like many tributaries joining and flowing together as a mighty river, diverse religions and cultures have combined to form the mighty river called India. What is a river but a confluence of its tributaries? The Ganga and the Indus, the two rivers that play a central role in the very definition of our civilisation and identity are made wide and deep by the coming together of so many tributaries. When we revere the Ganga at its widest expanse in the plains we recognise the many rivers and tributaries that over time and space join it. India, too, is defined similarly. A land of diversity, through time and space, where modern democracy has come to be built on the notion of pluralism and inclusiveness.

Admittedly, there are those even among us who do not share this syncretic view of India. They not only believe in the 'clash of civilisations' but also wish to encourage it. They do not, indeed cannot, represent the true spirit of our ancient land.

As Sunil Khilnani and Pratap Bhanu Mehta[1] have so eloquently argued in their thoughtful books, India's most important contribution to the world is the idea of syncretic pluralism that has

1 **Sunil Khilnani, *The Idea of India* (third edition, 2003) and Pratap Bhanu Mehta, *The Burden of Democracy* (2003).**

shaped the institutions of an inclusive democracy. I am aware of the scepticism expressed by Fareed Zakaria[2] about the 'illiberal' aspects of democracy. But with all our faults and limitations, with all the challenges and shortcomings, we have succeeded in stabilising representative democracy and ensuring the smooth transfer of power after every election at all levels of democratic representation in a country of continental dimensions with an electorate of over half a billion people.

That is the basis on which we can build a meaningful partnership with the world. We have, through history, approached the world as seekers of knowledge and opportunity. Indians have always reached out to the world as teachers and traders, as writers and workers, and never as conquerors.

The world has increasingly come to accept that open societies and open markets are the most natural and stable form of social and economic organisation. What is now increasingly clear is that an inclusive democracy, based on the principles of pluralism and multi-culturalism, is the most enduring means of dealing with the challenges posed by open markets and open societies.

The world community has been actively engaged in recent years in dealing with the perceived threat of globalisation and political extremism in its various manifestations, ranging from ethnic cleansing to jehadism.

There are no military solutions to such challenges. There are no unilateral solutions either. Any meaningful solution must be based on the principles of democratic pluralism and inclusivism; respect of the rule of law and of diversity of opinion and faith. The voice of moderation has to be empowered in all societies to make the world a better place to live in. The principle of an 'eye for an eye', as Gandhiji often reminded us, would leave us all blind.

Economists quantify our engagement with the world in terms of our share of world trade and capital flows, while strategic analysts look at military and political alliances. I submit to you for your

2 Fareed Zakaria, *The Future of Freedom: Illiberal Democracy at Home and Abroad* (2003).

consideration the idea that the most enduring engagement of a people with the world is through the realm of ideas and the idea we must engage the world through is the 'idea of India'; the idea of *Vasudhaiva kutumbakam.* The idea that even if nations may clash with one another, cultures and civilisations can coexist. The defining feature of the twenty-first century is not that it will be marked by a 'clash of civilisations', but that it will be shaped by a 'confluence of civilisations'.

I believe the world community can deal more meaningfully with the challenge of globalisation and the threat of terrorism by enabling a dialogue between nations and a 'confluence of civilisations'. India must actively engage the world towards this end.

By rejecting the politics of exclusion and voting in favour of the values of secularism and pluralism that we cherish, the people of India have once again given us reason to hold our head high in the comity of nations.

Those of us who celebrated the end of the Cold War and hoped to reach a development dividend from it are today dismayed by the new ideological divides that threaten global peace and prosperity. The ideology of a 'clash of civilisations' and of terrorism is a threat to world peace. We must empower the voices of moderation and of civilised discourse to enable a 'confluence of civilisations' to make the world a better and safer place to live in.

Just as many developed industrial economies assisted the so-called 'economies in transition' to make the transition from centrally planned economies to open market economies, the experience of a democracy like ours can be of some help in enabling the 'societies in transition' to evolve into open, inclusive, plural, democratic societies.

When the United Nations and governments of other democracies reach out to our Election Commission seeking its assistance in conducting elections we feel a sense of pride in our democratic processes and our institutions. Our Election Commission has no peer anywhere in the world. It has established an enviable record of efficiency and transparency in the conduct of elections from Kanyakumari to Kashmir.

Let me assure you that in putting forward my views on how we can contribute to the strengthening of democracy in the world, I am not advocating diplomatic activism nor would we in India ever advocate any form of political interventionism. Far from it. We recognise the sovereign right of every country to order its affairs in the manner most desired by its people. But I do believe that our experience can be of some help to the world community in its quest to strengthen the institutions of democracy and the idea of inclusive pluralism.

The partnership we seek and the basis of growth we wish to create should rest on this foundation of our commitment to the values of inclusive pluralism and multi-culturalism within the framework of an open society and an open economy. This is the promise our government has made at home. This is the experience we should happily share with the rest of the world. Our nationhood and our Republic are intrinsically linked to our commitment to democracy and our democracy has endured because we have enabled at home a dialogue between civilisations.

This is our message to the world and we should not shy away from opportunities to strengthen the institutions of democratic pluralism whenever we are called upon to do so. We know from our own experience that the world would be a safer place and growth and prosperity would be ensured if we can enable the 'confluence of civilisations' within the framework of democratic pluralism. The partnerships for growth that we can build on that basis will be truly enduring.

I think the time has come, as Panditji long believed, for India to, 'Come out of her shell and take full part in the life and activities of the modern age.'

I would be grateful to the people assembled here if you would consider some of these ideas and educate me whether I am correct to view our engagement with the world in these terms. I wish the conference all success and look forward to learning of its deliberations.

Moderator | **Vir Sanghvi**

Editorial Director, Hindustan Times

Manzar Khan (Sports Management Group International, London): If India is on the road to becoming an economic superpower what are the constraints and how we can level them out with our capabilities?

Dr Manmohan Singh: The most important thing that we have to do is to accelerate the tempo of social and economic change in our country and if our economy, in the years to come, grows at the rate of 7 to 8 per cent per annum – and I believe there is every reasonable expectation that it will – then the logic of compound interest itself will ensure that India will acquire a greater weightage in the world economy and in the processes that seek to resolve various international issues, whether these are regional fora or multilateral fora.

So, therefore, what happens to India will be determined by our commitment, by our ability to accelerate the tempo of social and economic change.

Q. How significant is peace and stability in South Asia?

Dr Manmohan Singh: South Asia is a subcontinent of great promise and great potential. It is unfortunate that because of various problems, to which I do not wish to refer to, the potential has not been fully utilised. If we have the wisdom and the courage to resolve all outstanding issues that bedevil us, I have every reason to believe that the future of this great subcontinent can change beyond recognition.

As I said earlier, we will make every effort to engage our neighbours in a cooperative arrangement to convert South Asia into a land of prosperity; a land in which the differences that may exist between various nations can be resolved through purposeful, negotiated, peaceful methods. That is our ambition. That is our hope.

Sanjay Trehan (Hindustan Times, New Delhi): You talked about the age of ideas and Winston Churchill also said that the future empires are going to be the empires of the mind. Do you have an action plan to unleash the creative potential of India, which quite often gets hemmed in by bureaucratic rigmarole?

Dr Manmohan Singh: The reforms of 1991 were part of a grand vision to liberate the Indian economy from the overhang of bureaucratic controls, which had for many decades suppressed the creativity of our people. That is one dimension. But establishing a market economy with equal concern for social equities is a great challenge that we face in our country.

We have to learn to become truly a knowledge society. For that we need a lot more commitment and emphasis on human resource development. Education is the most critical variable. We have to ensure that in the next ten years at least every school going child up to the age of fifteen or sixteen is in school.

We have a large number of institutions of higher learning – our IITs, our institutes of management – and we are very proud of their achievements. The information technology revolution has helped us convince the world that, given proper opportunities, we Indians are second to none when it comes to creativity and the exercise of a spirit of adventure and enterprise.

The challenge I see before our government and before our country is to create within our own country an atmosphere and environment in which the people of India do not have to go abroad to prove to the world that we are second to none. That is our ambition and that is, I hope, something which will excite the imagination of all our people.

Vir Sanghvi: It has now been several months since the elections, I think it is fair to say the Congress did not expect to be in office. It is probably fair to say you did not expect to be prime minister. You have had some months in the job now, what are your three biggest areas of concern in the months ahead?

Dr Manmohan Singh: Well I think my biggest area of concern right now is what we have stated in our Common Minimum Programme, that is, to give India's farmers a ray of hope. Our agriculture has had a raw deal in the last five or six years. Seventy per cent of our population lives in rural areas. They must get a feeling that they are equal partners in processes of development. That is our top priority.

Our second concern is the management of our infrastructure. India can grow at a much faster pace but our infrastructure, whether it consists of railways, ports, roads or the telecommunications setup, needs a quantum jump in terms of quantity and quality.

The third area of concern for our government is the human resource development dimension. Education and healthcare are two areas which are critical for the growth of our economy and they must, therefore, receive much greater attention than they have received.

Vir Sanghvi: What about the peace process? Is that a priority and how do you see it going?

Dr Manmohan Singh: I said earlier that South Asia is a subcontinent of great creativity. Somehow that creative potential has not been allowed to express itself because of various disputes that exist – principally disputes between India and Pakistan. We are committed to make an honest and sincere effort to resolve all outstanding disputes with Pakistan. The only condition is the commitment that was made by President Pervez Musharraf in January to Prime Minister Atal Behari Vajpayee that the territory of Pakistan will not be allowed to be used for cross-border terrorism. If that commitment is honoured in letter and spirit, we certainly have the will to engage Pakistan in a constructive dialogue to resolve all outstanding issues bilaterally – and that includes the issue of Jammu and Kashmir.

Our many diversities are cemented by secularism and a long tradition of tolerance. This makes us an example for a world where nations are torn apart by sectarian violence and conflicts ignited by religious and ethnic differences.

Democracy

And Progress

Sonia Gandhi

Sonia Gandhi

Chairperson, United Progressive Alliance

Sonia Gandhi was born on 9 December 1946 near Turin, Italy. While enrolled at a language school in Cambridge, England, she met Rajiv Gandhi, the elder son of Indira Gandhi, the then Prime Minister of India. They were married in 1968 and Sonia settled in India.

A pilot with Indian Airlines, Rajiv joined politics after the death of his younger brother Sanjay, in 1980, in a plane crash joined politics. Tragedy struck again with the assassination of Indira Gandhi in 1984. Her death catapulted Rajiv as the unopposed head of the Congress party. His subsequent landslide victory resulted in the largest electoral win ever for the party. But Rajiv himself was assassinated by a suicide bomber in 1991 – once again plunging the family into grief and the party into a crisis of leadership. In a replay of the aftermath of Mrs Gandhi's assassination, Sonia was offered the post of Party President and subsequently prime ministership. But the grieving Sonia declined.

For the next six years, Sonia Gandhi led a quiet life. But this was a difficult period for the Congress party. In the 1996 general elections, the Congress had its worst ever performance with just 28 per cent of the votes. Unable to ignore the decline, Sonia Gandhi decided to step into public life.

In the run up to the election this year, it was widely believed that Sonia Gandhi would be the next prime minister, should the Congress and its allies come to power. But she once again turned down the top post, nominating Dr Manmohan Singh instead while choosing to function both as the Party President and as Chairperson of the United Progressive Alliance.

Sonia continues to be the Chairperson of the Rajiv Gandhi Foundation; Indira Gandhi Memorial Trust; Jawaharlal Nehru Memorial Fund; Nehru Trust for Cambridge University; Nehru Memorial Museum and Library; and, Swaraj Bhawan Trust.

Sonia Gandhi has two children, Rahul and Priyanka.

THE *HINDUSTAN TIMES* HAS BEEN, OVER SEVERAL DECADES NOW, A DAILY HABIT OF LAKHS OF READERS. WITH THIS LEADERSHIP INITIATIVE IT HAS ALSO BECOME AN instrument for stimulating thought and reflection outside its columns. This is an occasion for many of us to step back from the preoccupations of our daily lives and reflect on larger and more crucial issues.

We met exactly, a year ago to discuss India and South Asia and I bet none of you had expected me to be here today as part of the establishment rather than the Opposition.

Today, we assemble to look at India and the world.

The two are interlinked. India has many security concerns that are real and cannot be wished away. Even so, India can, must and, I am sure, will take the lead to build an enduring political and economic partnerships with her neighbours. This is an essential prerequisite for an India occupying its rightful place on the world stage.

Enormous, defining and fundamental changes are taking place in the world with astonishing rapidity. One might ask, has it not always been so? In living memory, in the life of India as a new and independent nation-state, our predecessors have had to deal with situations which demanded of them high statesmanship and courage. Jawaharlal Nehru, Lal Bahadur Shastri, Indira Gandhi and Rajiv Gandhi all faced a world where India's place was far from secure and its interests were constantly under assault. They steered our nation through the hostility of a bipolar world and threats and wars in our neighbourhood.

The challenges we face now are, of course, of a different kind. The old conflicts between nation-states and between blocks of nation-states have yielded to the growing menace of terrorism. This is an enemy where the distinction between state and non-state actors is sometimes blurred. This is an enemy that recognises no borders and has no identifiable geographical limitations. At the same time, the familiar world order of the second half of the twentieth century has given place to a disturbing imbalance for which traditional institutional mechanisms, such as the United Nations, appear to be ill-prepared and ill-suited. Technological advance is spectacular but the benefits are unevenly distributed both within and among nations.

What is India's place in such a world in the coming years?

Obviously, that place has to be based on the tripod of democracy, diversity and development that has sustained our nation and our people these past decades. India's external strength depends on her internal cohesiveness. The fulfilment of India's global ambitions rests on the edifice of domestic harmony. If India wants to be seen as being exclusive in the world, as she indeed is, then she has to be inclusive at home. Our nationalism has necessarily to be secular, pluralistic and liberal as bequeathed to us by Mahatma Gandhi, Rabindranath Tagore and Jawaharlal Nehru. We cannot manifest vigour and independence in our relationships with other nations or exercise influence in the world, if we are not strong and cohesive at home.

The remarkable resilience of our democracy, vividly displayed in these past few months, gives us a voice that is heard and respected throughout the world. Speaking of resilience, I am glad to see that the voter turnout in the world's most powerful democracy is, at last, comparable to the turnout in the world's most populous democracy. Our many diversities are cemented by secularism and a long tradition of tolerance. This makes us an example for a world where nations are torn apart by sectarian violence and conflicts ignited by religious and ethnic differences. Our sustained commitment to development has yielded impressive results. Even though we have much more to accomplish, our economic and social transformation over the past half-century cannot be denied.

We are a democratic nation of a billion people living harmoniously in a pluralistic society. We constitute one of the fastest growing economies in the world. Our credentials can hardly be doubted. Yet, I find it difficult to comprehend that the world is still treated to a regime of groupings based on the Second World War's outcomes of victory and defeat. The UN Security Council, as now constituted, for instance, is not just unrepresentative, it is unintelligent.

A global role brings with it global responsibilities. Traditionally, we have always advocated the cause of multi-lateralism in world affairs. We have always championed the strengthening of the United Nations. However, new concerns have emerged. We must take note of them seriously and fashion effective and credible responses in areas like climate change, environment, child labour and HIV/AIDS.

As we look ahead, what will drive India's relationship with the world?

India's potential for what has come to be broadly called outsourcing is imparting a whole new dimension to our global links.

New opportunities are opening up.

As the world ages, for instance, India's capacity to provide health services, both in modern and traditional medicine is being recognised. International media organisations are beginning to use India as their base. India has emerged as the preferred destination for research and development and for an expanding range of services. Our hard work, the technological skills of our young women and men, our ability to talk to the world in its preferred languages, both alphabetic and binary, and the sheer innate enterprise of our people have given us a singular opportunity that will, I believe – I know – be the driving force of our role in the world.

In addition, there are other factors that would determine the nature and depth of our interaction.

First, quite clearly the quest for energy security will be paramount. Even as we intensify oil and gas exploration efforts at home, we will need to develop long-term, cost-effective sources of supply to meet our growing demand. India has emerged as a major investor in different countries like Russia, Sudan, Vietnam, Myanmar, West Africa – a region that has been somewhat peripheral to India's world-view – has emerged as being important to us. Central Asia offers growing possibilities. And opportunities abound in our own region itself.

Second, Indian companies will expand their global presence. This is already happening not only in terms of our exports but, more importantly, in terms of investment. There was a time when our presence was culinary. Some years back, while referring to the perceived threat of racial conflict, *The Economist*, I believe, wrote that Britain would not drown in rivers of blood but in oceans of curry.

Today, besides these oceans of delicious mouth-watering curries we have a growing number of Indian firms in diverse areas like IT, pharmaceuticals, textiles, petrochemicals, steel and engineering proudly planting their flags all over the world. As we seek and receive increased foreign investment, our vibrant private and public sector will also emerge as major investors abroad.

Third, India will also become a much sought-after provider of development assistance. Here again, on the one hand, we will be the recipients of foreign aid in niche areas although we now repay much more than what we receive. But, on the other hand, we will also be a supplier of both technical and financial assistance. Thus far we have focused largely on countries in our immediate neighbourhood but there is no question that as India grows and builds its economic capability it will look at many other countries as well.

Fourth, the common perception that India will be just the services capital of the world will change as she begins to revitalise her vast manufacturing industries. As and when the advanced countries reduce their huge farm subsidies, Indian farmers will also begin to make their presence felt in global markets. A country that was written off as a basket case four decades ago now has the capacity to feed the world, thanks largely to the vision and determination of Indira Gandhi.

Finally, India will carve out a new and creative relationship with people of Indian origin living overseas. So many of them, as you all know, have distinguished themselves in different fields. Some of them have even been elected presidents and prime ministers. Just a few days ago, an Indian American was elected to the US House of Representatives.

The ancestors of Bharat Jagdeo, the President of Guyana, hailed from – guess where – village Thakurain-ka-Purva in my old constituency, Amethi.

India-born scientists and technologists, authors and doctors are celebrated but we also have around three million workers in West

Asia who are remitting at best $6-$7 billion of their savings annually. There can be no doubt that the expertise of the Indian community abroad is waiting to be harnessed to accelerate our own development and also to forge new friendships for us across the globe.

So far I have focused largely on economics, trade and investment. But India has a pivotal role to play in the global fight against terrorism about which I spoke a little while ago. It will also be central to any global effort to contain the threat posed by the spread of nuclear, chemical and biological weapons. Terrorism cannot, and should not – must not – be dealt with in a selective and segmented manner within the framework of individual nation-states and their priorities. And the approach that says 'the terrorism I face is of higher priority than the terrorism you face' has dangerous implications for global stability and security.

India still faces numerous development challenges. How successfully we address these challenges in basic areas like literacy, education, health and infrastructure, for example, depends on ourselves and ourselves alone. But economic integration with the world in a manner determined by us will undoubtedly help the economy expand even faster. This is essential for generating more jobs and eliminating mass poverty and as we look at India and the world let us not, even for a moment, overlook this reality. While, we celebrate our achievements, let us not forget that many tasks await our focused attention, particularly in rural India where two out of every three of our countrymen and women live and work. India's interaction and integration with the world must always keep these basics in mind so that *all* Indians have equal opportunities and live a life of dignity and fulfilment.

In conclusion, let me emphasise that India has always had a universal perspective. That perspective has been mutually rewarding and enriching. Many more opportunities await us. Many more horizons beckon. I have no doubt that we will move forward with self-confidence knowing that ultimately it is not just our potential but, more importantly, our performance that will get us the position we desire and deserve.

Moderator | **Vir Sanghvi**

Editorial Director, Hindustan Times

Chinmoy Gharekhan (Former Indian Ambassador to the UN): Nearly six months have gone by since your historic statement in which you renounced the office to which you were rightfully entitled. That renunciation went down, of course, greatly with our people and also across the world. I wonder if you have anything to share with us about what went on in your mind at that time.

Sonia Gandhi: Well, I have stated before that my aim has never been to occupy the prime ministerial chair. My aim has always been to strengthen the Congress party and, in doing so, defeating the anti-secular forces which were in government. Now if I was to speak to you about what went through my mind in those few days or hours I think I would have to fill a couple of chapters of a book and, therefore, I think you will have to wait for that book.

Vir Sanghvi: Had you always made up your mind or was it something you decided after the election?

Sonia Gandhi: Well I had already decided; always knew that I would never occupy that chair.

Vir Sanghvi: Really, right from the beginning?

Sonia Gandhi: Right from the beginning. You know, but sometimes the flesh is weak.

Pankaj Vohra (Senior Journalist): Many people consider you to be the power behind the throne, do you agree with the assumption?

Sonia Gandhi: When I was offered, elected, to occupy that very chair of power, positional power, why would I want to be the power behind the throne.

The story that I am the power behind the throne dates back to the days when Rajiv Gandhi was the Prime Minister. At that time

I was supposed to have sacked ministers, brought in new ones, decided on whom the Prime Minister should meet and not meet, so I am quite used to it.

Vir Sanghvi: So, you are not the power behind the throne?

Sonia Gandhi: No, I am not the power behind the throne, I do not wish to be the power behind the throne.

Vir Sanghi: But do you look at government files? Do you make any of those decisions?

Sonia Gandhi: No, I do not look at government files. I do not take government decisions. Well, first we have a Congress party manifesto, then we have the Common Minimum Programme, which includes portions of our manifesto and programmes of other political parties in coalition with us. So, government policy and programmes are based on documents. There is nothing really major that needs to be discussed and if ever there is anything, you know, one can always do so. We do meet with the Prime Minister, a few of us from the party on a weekly basis, just to exchange notes and to discuss what is going on.

Vir Sanghvi: Would you go and see him or does he come and see you?

Sonia Gandhi: No, I would not allow him to come and see me. I always go and see him. I think that is the right way.

Phiroz Vandrewala (Executive Vice President, Tata Consultancy Services): As the convenor of the UPA, how do you see yourself dealing with the conflicts of coalition politics, the tug of war with the Left?

Sonia Gandhi: We have a coalition government. Our coalition partners are our valued allies. When we worked on the Common Minimum Programme they were all consulted and that document represents programmes and policies that they wanted to be included.

You mentioned the Left, they do speak out, and I believe it is the right of any coalition partner to do so. We sit down in a very civil fashion and discuss issues and come to certain agreements or understandings. For the Congress party, this is a new experiment; a new experience at the Centre. Of course, we have coalitions and have worked with coalitions at the state level but it is really the first time that we are working in a coalition framework at the Centre. So, there are bound to be hiccups and we have to learn. I do not think we have done that badly. It has only been six months and there has not been any major hassle. We tend to have a very short memory but if you were to think of the previous government – of the problems, of the tamashas, which were going on at that time, every now and then you know, so-called interlocutors were rushed to the south of India or to the Northeast to pacify one coalition partner or another – and compare our position to that we have not done badly at all. And I can assure you, we will continue to work together.

Scott Bayman (President & CEO, GE-India): Now that President Bush has been re-elected, what suggestions would you have for the US to take the relationship forward with India?

Sonia Gandhi: Well first of all I would like to congratulate President Bush. India has worked with him and his administration for the last four years and will continue to do so. Yes, we would like him to be concerned about our security concerns but these are matters which will be discussed at the government level. We have developed a good rapport and relationship with the US and we are going to work to maintain it, sustain it and even improve it.

Imran Khan (Founder, Tehreek-e-Insaf): Do you make a distinction between a freedom struggle and terrorism?

Sonia Gandhi: Now, that is a tough one. You are referring to our eternal problem, of course. As you know the Congress party has from the beginning been encouraging the previous government to initiate a dialogue with Pakistan. While earlier they were not keen to do so, eventually they listened to us and initiated a dialogue. The dialogue continues under our government. When we ourselves were asking the previous government to initiate the dialogue, then we are going to see to it that it continues and work towards finding a solution to our problem.

S.K. Singh (Former Foreign Secretary): You mentioned your constituency in Uttar Pradesh. I too am from the state. How do you, as the Congress President, find the situation in our state? I find it rather dismal.

Sonia Gandhi: I agree with you, I find it dismal as well.

S.K. Singh: But you can do something about it. I can't.

Sonia Gandhi: I am disappointed with the situation of the Congress party in Uttar Pradesh and I have thought about it and I think about it almost day and night. What can we do to change the situation in Uttar Pradesh, which is so vital to the Congress party? I think within the next two days and hopefully thereafter, things will start picking up in Uttar Pradesh.

Vir Sanghvi: That means only one thing: you are about to appoint somebody. Are you? Are you going to change things in Uttar Pradesh. Make new appointments, is that what you are hinting at?

Sonia Gandhi: Yes, I am planning to do so. Yes.

Vir Sanghvi: So, can we expect an announcement in the next couple of days?

Sonia Gandhi: Yes, definitely.

D.R. Karthikeyan (Special Director, Retd, CBI): In recent years, the condition of rural India, particularly farmers, has become pathetic. Thousands of farmers have been forced to commit suicide. Shouldn't something be done for the farmers? Related to this is the question of water. Water is going to be the biggest constraint on development. On these two issues what are the time-bound steps your government will take?

Sonia Gandhi: Yes, you have pointed out two most serious problems. Farmers have had a very raw deal during the previous government's terms. But one of the first actions of our Prime Minister was to look at the problems faced by farmers and allocate a huge amount of money to strengthen the agricultural sector.

On the other issue, I am sure you are aware that the Prime Minister has set up groups of ministers to look specifically into how to contain the water problem within a certain specific period of time so that every village in India has water.

Kanwar Khalid Younis (Member of Parliament, MQM, Pakistan): South Asia has a tradition of keeping and grooming inherited politics. Do you have a soft corner for Rahul and Priyanka?

Sonia Gandhi: Well they are my son and daughter and so, yes, I have a soft corner for them.

Abhishek Misra (Head of Marketing, Unitech Group): Many of us expected Rahul Gandhi to get a party post. Do you plan to do that?

Sonia Gandhi: My son Rahul is, as you all know, a member of Parliament. He is now concentrating on looking after his constituency, my old constituency. I think he has to gain some experience both at looking after his constituency and also of the organisation of the Congress party.

Vir Sanghvi: And Priyanka?

Sonia Gandhi: Priyanka is a wife and a mother of two very small children and at the moment she is fully concentrating on her family and does not intend to participate actively in politics.

Omar Abdullah (President, National Conference): My question is in two parts. The first is on a personal level and has to do with the way in which you have evolved both as a leader and as a person. How did this transformation come about? The other question, refers to what you said right in the beginning, nobody expected you to be part of the ruling establishment. But you are. So obviously, there is something in the blueprint for partnership and growth that the NDA had which was wrong and the people did not appreciate. What is in your blueprint for the UPA for partnership and growth that is different from theirs and how do you plan to go about achieving it?

Sonia Gandhi: The difference between the NDA and UPA came alive vividly during our election campaign. Their slogan was 'India Shining'. Ours is *'Aam aadmi ke liye, Congress party aam aadmi ke saath hai'*. So, I think that explains it all. Besides we are for a secular India; we are for pluralistic India; we are for a liberal India. As regard to your other question, I think I have learnt from many, including you.

India and Pakistan

Partnership for Peace

and Prosperity

■

Imran Khan

■

Farooq Abdullah

■

Moderator

Rajdeep Sardesai

Managing Editor, NDTV

Imran Khan

Founder, Tehreek-e-Insaf, Pakistan

Born Imran Khan Niazi into a Pathan family of landowners on 25 November 1952 in Lahore, Khan is probably the finest cricketer from Pakistan. An outstanding all-rounder, he became a national hero when he captained the Pakistani cricket team to victory and brought back the World Cup in the 1992 which took place in Australia.

Khan grew up in Lahore and was educated at Aitchison College, Lahore, and subsequently the Royal Grammar School in Worcester and the Keble College, Oxford.

He captained the Oxford University cricket team and played for Worcestershire and then Sussex. He captained Pakistan from 1982 till 1988, when he decided to quit cricket while he was still at the top of his career.

The then Pakistan President General Zia-ul-Haq appealed to Khan to rejoin the team as it needed his expertise and leadership, Khan returned to the cricketing world, only to bring back the only ever World Cup trophy to Pakistan in 1992.

Since giving up cricket, Khan has devoted his time to raising funds for the Shaukat Khanum Memorial Cancer Clinic in memory of his late mother.

In 1996, Khan founded the Tehreek-e-Insaf (Movement for Justice) party and had to face an election that neither he nor his party was prepared for. The party failed to win a single seat, but ever since, Khan has been at the helm of a crusade against corruption and injustice in Pakistan. He is counted among the few Pakistani politicians who have had the courage to challenge the validity of Pakistan's military establishment.

Khan has two sons, Suleiman Issa and Qassim.

Dr Farooq Abdullah

Former Chief Minister, Jammu and Kashmir

The only son of Kashmir's most influential leader, Sheikh Abdullah, Farooq Abdullah was elected President of the National Conference (NC) in March 1981.

Though elected to Parliament, Farooq was called to serve as the Health Minister in his father's state government later that same year. In September 1981 following the death of Sheikh Abdullah, Farooq was appointed Chief Minister of Jammu and Kashmir. In 1983, he called for fresh assembly elections, winning with a massive margin.

Farooq's first trial by fire took place in 1984 when his government was dismissed and his estranged brother-in-law, G. M. Shah was installed as Chief Minister with Congress support. The government fell when the Congress withdrew support and President's rule imposed. In November 1986, Farooq entered into an electoral alliance with Rajiv Gandhi's Congress, won the elections and returned to the state as Chief Minister.

But the years that followed saw the emergence of militancy in the state. In May that year, Farooq's motorcade was attacked while he was on his way to a mosque. This was the first of many direct attacks against him. By 1989, with terrorist activities showing no signs of abating, paramilitary forces had to be deployed to maintain law and order in the state.

President's rule had to be imposed once again as Farooq was forced to step down as Chief Minister. In 1996, Farooq returned to power as fresh assembly elections were held. This time around, however, he entered into an alliance with the BJP-led United Front government. His son, Omar Abdullah, was appointed a Minister of State in the Central Government but resigned in the aftermath of communal riots in Gujarat. Later, Farooq announced that he was stepping down as NC President, appointing his son in his place.

Throughout his political career, Farooq has campaigned for Kashmir to remain within the Indian union. But he has also campaigned for greater autonomy and more central aid to the state.

Farooq and his wife, Molly have a son and three daughters.

RAJDEEP SARDESAI: WELCOME TO WHAT COULD BE THE MOST INTERESTING SESSION SIMPLY BECAUSE WE WOULD BE TALKING TO TWO MOST INTERESTING POLITICIANS THAT YOU could find at this moment in India and Pakistan.

If you've been to any Indo-Pak seminar recently you'll know the buzz phrase is 'out-of-the-box'. Fortunately we have Farooq Abdullah and Imran Khan in their own way 'out-of-the-box' politicians. It is very rare that a Pakistani cricket captain would actually give up the rules of the game to play politics. It is equally true that Farooq Abdullah is an unconventional politician. And we will focus on 'out-of-the-box' solutions to the Indo-Pak impasse.

My first proposal: let us put a moratorium for the next twenty years on the Kashmir issue.

Imran Khan: The problem is that as long as you do not solve the Kashmir issue and just push it under the carpet which, in effect, is what a moratorium will accomplish – extremists on both sides of the border will not let matters rest. Any incident in Kashmir will be used to further their narrow agendas. The issue has to be faced and it has to be faced head on. It needs visionary leadership.

In my opinion, the people are ready. I just watched the Pakistan-India series a few months ago and I cannot tell you the response on the cricket field and outside, when the Indian team went to the bazaars and to restaurants, and the way they were treated.

The people of the subcontinent, specially the younger generation, have come to the conclusion that this issue has to be solved. They are ready for it. The problem is that the leadership does not seem to have the vision and the decision-making power to solve this issue.

Farooq Abdullah: Well, I think it is not a bad idea (to have a moratorium). If our roadmap is towards trade, economic progress, getting together and the vision of Indira Gandhi for SAARC (South Asian Association for Regional Cooperation), fundamentalism on both sides of the border must die. What has really held SAARC back is the India-Pakistan trouble, otherwise SAARC would have become like the European Union common market, moving towards the day when we would have one currency and a joint Parliament of all these countries.

A moratorium would give time to people to calm down and cool temperatures. Militancy is called a war for liberation but has actually become a way of earning money.

The problem will not go away with a moratorium but we will achieve some measure of progress. For instance, when the Indians went to Pakistan, I could not go. I am the President of the Jammu and Kashmir Cricket Association and when I requested the President of the BCCI[1] to go to Lahore, the answer from Pakistan's Ministry of Interior was, 'Please don't bring Farooq Abdullah.'

A twenty-year moratorium would give us space during which we would probably grow to understand each other better. Personal bitterness would probably die. I think that might give us hope. I don't say the Kashmir problem will die, but at least a new generation and new thinking will be there, which will probably create better understanding between these two nations. It is just a question of time.

Rajdeep Sardesai: Twenty-five years ago when India played Pakistan in cricket, Imran Khan, you were amongst those who said that cricket between the two countries was like a war without weapons. Have things changed and do you believe that cricket can break barriers?

Imran Khan: When I first came to play in India in 1979, I received the sort of hospitality that the Indian visitors and the Indian cricket team saw this time round in Pakistan. Bearing in mind that only a year earlier, the two armies were facing each other on the border and the level of hatred across the border, the change is bizarre.

But I do see a change in the thinking of the people. I think people have realised that this issue cannot be solved through arms and this (realisation) is mutual. So, if it cannot be solved through war then people have accepted that this is going to be a long-drawn process but one that has to be solved through dialogue. This is a very positive thing.

Once that realisation has happened, I do not see why the leadership in the two countries does not have the ability to rise above

---

1 Board of Control for Cricket in India.

petty politics and their own constituencies and try and tackle it? There have been far more difficult issues than Kashmir that have been sorted out. I remember playing in the seventies and eighties with South African cricketers in County cricket in England where every South African cricketer told me that if Apartheid was dismantled, South Africa would descend into bloodshed. It took two visionary leaders, Nelson Mandela and F. W. de Clerk to solve the issue and carry the people with them.

One way of thinking is that a moratorium will somehow cool tempers. But there is no guarantee. Consider the situation, what guarantee do we have that governments won't generate hatred on the Kashmir issue to win elections? In my opinion this is an issue that should be tackled head on.

The people of the subcontinent, have come to the problem is that the leadership does not seem to have the

Farooq Abdullah: Imran, suppose you are the prime minister of Pakistan and I am the prime minister of India and we are sitting across the table, what will you tell me?

Imran Khan: Well ...

Farooq Abdullah: Frankly because one day you will be prime minister. Whether I am or not is a different matter.

Imran Khan: I once asked your son, 'Look I know your public stance. But what is your private stance?' He was very careful and did not really give in.

I feel very strongly that the solution to Kashmir lies with the people of Kashmir. The only way you can solve the issue is by allowing the genuine representatives of Kashmir to come forward to sit down and talk to Pakistan and India, the two other parties. These three parties must decide the issue. Now, how do you get the genuine representatives of people of Kashmir? I think first the area has to be demilitarised. Second, you have to hold elections that are considered free and fair where people can come to vote. By the way, I say the same thing in my own country about free and fair elections. It's possible that you have to hold the elections in Kashmir under the United Nations. Whatever leadership that emerges from Kashmir should then decide what to do. I think that is the only just and lasting solution.

Farooq Abdullah: That is you as the prime minister. I as the prime minister, on the other hand, would say let us open the frontiers. Let people come and go. Let them see what is on the other side and over the years this will bring about change. What has been publicised for a long time is that the prayers are not being held in the mosques; that the mosques are closed; that there is genocide. This (propaganda) will disappear once there is people-to-people contact. Only then can we go to the next stage of finding a solution through the people.

conclusion that the Kashmir issue has to be solved. The vision and the decision-making power to solve this issue.

– Imran Khan

Rajdeep Sardesai: But Dr Abdullah when you were Chief Minister you never gave any of these suggestions. It is much easier for you to raise these solutions when you are an Opposition politician.

Farooq Abdullah: The problem was that I was fighting terrorism. Innocent people were being killed and made answerable to terrorists. But they (the terrorists) are not my gods. They don't decide whether I pray or don't; I fast or don't; I wear a veil or don't. Who the hell are they? I have to face God and they too have to do that. Then, there will be no king or poor man. They don't tell me what is the way of Islam. I am a Muslim. There is no doubt that I am a Muslim who believes that God is my judge and, therefore, no one else can judge me.

That is what I was fighting when I was the chief minister. I was fighting with the people who try to impose something that does not exist.

Rajdeep Sardesai: Let us come to the second out-of-the-box-solution: suppose we have soft borders and allow free contact between Pakistanis

and Indians. Imran Khan, would you support a soft border where Kashmir becomes a bridge between India and Pakistan rather than a divide?

Imran Khan: I agree with Dr Abdullah's solutions with regard to people-to-people contact. I think the more people get to know each other, the more they realise that they don't have to demonise one another. Ignorance makes it easier to demonise the other side.

Rajdeep Sardesai: Are you ready to conceive that what is happening in Kashmir today may not necessarily be a freedom struggle?

Imran Khan: When I asked Mrs Sonia Gandhi the question (on how to distinguish between terrorism and freedom fighters)[2], it was not limited to Kashmir. It was a reference to George Bush's war on terrorism. Unless you distinguish between a freedom struggle and terrorism, you will end up creating more terrorists. The Americans have spent $400 billion on their war against terror, but is the world a safer place? Is there less terrorism now? Can anyone say that there won't be another attack on the US or there won't be more attacks anywhere else?

You just have to look back and know that terrorism cannot be sorted out if you do not make that distinction. I don't say that I am an expert on Kashmir who knows who are the terrorists and who are the freedom fighters. All I know is that the people of Pakistan – who I do know – and the people in India – or what I know of them – want an end to it. You cannot keep pushing it under the carpet and thinking something will happen someday. It does not work like that. If the people are ready today, why can the leadership not tackle the issue?

Rajdeep Sardesai: But the two of you, in a sense, form that leadership. Should India also abandon its stand that Kashmir is an integral part of India?

Dr Farooq Abdullah: I have grown up in India where there are a number of religions. We are like a garden with many flowers of different colours. I cannot live in a situation where I am asked to

2 Please refer to Chapter 2: Democracy and Progress.

choose a garden with only one flower. It will suffocate me and I will die.

My state has people of all religions. Terrorism drew the Hindus out. That is the tragedy of our state. I wish you could come to Kashmir and see those people and the tragedy of their lives. I would rather die than see the people further divided. I would prefer to find a solution without going through the trauma of another division. I was not responsible for 1947. The leaders responsible for 1947 must pay for it one day as this nation is paying for it now.

Today, the people of countries like Germany and England – once great enemies – can cross in and out and work in each other's country. I hope a similar day will come for us and no division takes place anymore.

Imran Khan: Dr Abdullah let me just say one thing. As far as I have read the Quran, I do not understand how anyone could interpret it by making it exclusive and where you say that other religions cannot flourish. You have to look back at the history of Islam to what we consider to be the Golden Period to see the level of tolerance, which just did not exist in the rest of the world, and people were allowed to practice their own faith.

There is an injunction in the Quran that you cannot demolish anyone's place of worship because God lives everywhere. I do not understand the Taliban-type of Islam. I understand what you say about ethnic cleansing in Kashmir. Look at the bloodshed that went on between Germany and England, Germany and France. But they could resolve issues and come up with solutions.

So what I am saying is that it is possible that the people of Kashmir might not want to join Pakistan or India and may want an autonomous place. The country, which I feel we should look to is Switzerland. Here is a country that has a population the size of Lahore. It has twenty-five cantons and every canton is semi-autonomous. The people feel they are the masters of their lives.

Perhaps that is what the Kashmiris might want. But let their representatives take a decision. I think it is the only just solution.

You are saying that you don't want another big split. There might not be one. As Dr Manmohan Singh has said, India is moving fast with an 8 per cent growth rate and becoming a superpower. Perhaps other countries might want to become part of India in another ten to fifteen years.

Rajdeep Sardesai: Is it possible to have a concept of joint sovereignty? It has been tried in some European countries. Would you support it, Dr Abdullah?

Farooq Abdullah: No, I would not support it. Why not have soft borders instead? We have autonomy, maximum autonomy. Why can we not think of this solution rather than joint sovereignty, independent sections or dividing it further into seven regions and then making a greater Kashmir? Why all this when there is a simple solution without further hurting the sentiments of Indians and Pakistanis?

Let us open the frontiers. Let people come and go. Let years, this will bring change.

Rajdeep Sardesai: Your suggest that the line of control (LoC) becomes a permanent border between the two countries and it is a soft border that allows people from two countries to freely travel across it ...

Farooq Abdullah: Travel, trade, marry, live in whatever comfort they can, why not? I would love Pakistanis to come and eat as much meat as they want (in Kashmir). I would love to open casinos so that they can gamble as much as they want rather than go to Beirut or somewhere else. I would love Imran to come and play golf and cricket in Kashmir.

Rajdeep Sardesai: Mr Khan do you really believe that there are domestic constituencies in the two countries that would be ready for that? Would a domestic constituency in Pakistan be ready for the LoC as a permanent border? Would Pakistan give up its claim to the Valley and allow soft borders and would India give up its claims to Pakistan occupied Kashmir (PoK)?

Imran Khan: I still think that you and I have no right to decide the destiny of the people of Kashmir. They must take their own decisions.
Rajdeep Sardesai: Will Pakistan accept it?

Imran Khan: Yes, I think if you have a leader who has credibility and the support of the people. People will follow such a leader because they want a solution.

Rajdeep Sardesai: Does the General (Pervez Musharraf) have that credibility?

Imran Khan: No. But let us wait for the next elections.

Rajdeep Sardesai: The other view is that India as the larger country has to be far more generous and accommodating and that India must take the first major steps. You cannot expect Pakistan to be proactive. A few weeks ago, General Musharraf suggested demilitarization but India's response was that we will not discuss this matter through the media. We talk of out-of-the-box solutions but we want to stay in the box.

them see what is on the other side and, over the

– Farooq Abdullah

Farooq Abdullah: One of the first things we have to create is trust which does not exist. I don't think any prime minister could have done what Atal Behari Vajpayee did to go to shake the hands of the Pakistanis. And yet plans for Kargil were already underway.

I saw Kargil at a very close range. I went there while the battle was being fought. Soldiers from the other side were killed but they (Pakistanis) refused to accept that they were their soldiers.

So, I think Imran we have to create a sense of trust before the Indian government or Indian people accept any further positive move. I think the first steps have already been taken with trade barriers being lifted and freer access to information and press. That sort of a thing will go away only when we have further mutual understanding. Your people will come; our people will go. We will shoot films. Your lovely people will come here – maybe some marriages will take place. I am looking forward to that.

Rajdeep Sardesai: Imran, can people-to-people contact really break barriers or are both of you essentially living in denial that we are two countries that are finding it extremely difficult to live with each other?

Imran Khan: I agree with what Farooq Abdullah is saying. Where I differ is that I still feel it is the leadership that will eventually decide what will happen.

Look, you know I am a critic of General Musharraf and I am in the Opposition, but I have to say that he seems sincere. He is going out of his way to make these statements. He has been roasted at home, by the way, for shifting from the Security Council resolution position, saying that we could actually be flexible. He got a lot of criticism. Somehow after the Kargil misadventure – which I don't, I can't and will never attempt to defend – there is a realisation that there is no military solution and he sincerely wants to move on the Kashmir talks.

He really has stuck his neck out and I think there should be a response from India. The dialogue should proceed now; the leadership should be bolder. And as a bigger country that is aspiring to be a superpower and should rightly be in the Security Council as the world's biggest democracy, India should take the initiative.

Rajdeep Sardesai: Let me just get a final word from Farooq Abdullah on the trust factor. Can Imran Khan and Farooq Abdullah trust each other and, more importantly, can the two governments learn to trust each other?

Farooq Abdullah: As Imran said it depends on the leadership. As long as terrorist camps are in operation by one general or another or by one force or another, for as long as extremism is existent, it will take time to come up with a solution for Kashmir. It will take time to build trust.

Rajdeep Sardesai: So you're saying an end to violence is a precondition to a move forward.

Farooq Abdullah: All violence. And then you have to start building brick by brick.

Rajdeep Sardesai: And you Imran are saying that India has to be seen to be more flexible to the average Pakistani.

Imran Khan: Also, to lay such a precondition is to sabotage it. You only need a few people to throw a few bombs and the whole thing will fall apart. It is exactly the argument Ariel Sharon uses with the

Palestinian leadership: first stop all violence and then talk. But they are not going to talk.

Putting the mission and the vision ahead of the self, that is what you need in the subcontinent. Unfortunately we have not had quality leadership and I would, by the way, praise Mr Vajpayee. I agree with Dr Abdullah, he did come to Pakistan and I do feel that he was sincere. I thought he took very bold initiatives and I think that we should keep going on.

Farooq Abdullah: I would remind this audience of Yitzhak Rabin, Prime Minister of Israel. When he went to the White House there were two enemies, Rabin and Yasser Arafat, and I remember his words: 'We have spilt blood, we are both the ones who are fighting on the other side. The time has come when this blood letting must stop and we must make a fresh start.' Imran, this is what I repeat of that great man who gave his life. Maybe Ariel Sharon does not follow it but one day it will happen. I hope Omar (Abdullah) will be able to see the day when India and Pakistan will find that blood letting is over and friendship develops. Imran, let us hope and pray that the day does come.

Moderator | **Rajdeep Sardesai**

Managing Editor, NDTV

General V.P. Malik (Former Chief of Army Staff): My question is addressed to Imran Khan and it is on that very important issue he raised about making a distinction between freedom fighters and terrorists.

I would like to ask you, how will you differentiate between people who are trying to kill innocent people in your mosques or on the streets or even Pervez Musharraf and those who are attacking elected representatives in state assemblies and in Parliament? Would you consider them freedom fighters or would you consider them terrorists?

Imran Khan: It is very straight-forward. There is no dispute regarding people who attack state assemblies, mosques and kill children (they are terrorists). The problem arises in defining the people who are fighting the US occupation in Iraq, who are fighting against a war that Kofi Annan has called illegal. The US says the people who are fighting American soldiers are terrorists.

What is happening in Chechenya? Twenty per cent of the population has been killed and thousands of Chechens have been driven out of their homes. When they fight Russian soldiers and harm them, they are considered freedom fighters amongst the Chechens themselves.

It is when there are double standards that problems arise. You know that the CIA had set up training camps in Pakistan to train guerillas to fight the Soviet Union in Afghanistan. They were called the *Mujahideen* and glamorised because they were against foreign occupation. We all looked upon them as heroes. The very same people today are hunted as terrorists.

What is the solution? I feel that the way to fight terrorism is to strengthen international institutions like the UN. I think it needs to be reformed and I don't think that the elite club should grow. I think the UN should be democratised. There should be some basis for why people should have a vote. I feel that a country that has elections along with an independent judicial system should be allowed to vote and that the assembly should then decide what is terrorism and what is a fight for freedom.

You have to strengthen international institutions and you cannot have unilateral action. There should not be one state that has the right to be the judge, jury and executioner because that then breeds more terrorism.

Omar Abdullah (President, National Conference): Mr Imran Khan you said that the leadership on both sides will decide how Jammu and Kashmir is to be resolved.

Very little has been spoken in this discussion about the wishes of the Kashmiri people. I would be interested to know from both panelists how they feel the wishes of the Kashmiri people can be ascertained. General Musharraf has suggested that solutions unacceptable to India and Pakistan could be left out but did not mention anything about solutions unacceptable to the people of Jammu and Kashmir. My question is that if you leave out solutions unacceptable to India and Pakistan, are you left with any solution and, if you are, could either of you suggest what that possible solution could be?

Imran Khan: For me the only solution is to have credible elections. Credible elections mean those that are acceptable to everyone by neutral umpires, perhaps the United Nations. Whatever leadership emerges that would be representative of the people of Kashmir.

Farooq Abdullah: Well, he has seen the elections in Pakistan and has suffered because of it. We've also seen the elections in Florida. We have had elections in Jammu and Kashmir whereas there has been no election in as far as Azad Kashmir or the northern territories. Let us first get things moving in the right direction through people-to-people contact.

I would like to share with you one thing which I have never said before. My father was hoping that the Rawalpindi road would be opened. In 1974 when I met Prime Minister Bhutto, I told him, 'If you ask me, don't open the road.' He said, 'Why not?' I replied, 'Because if you open the road the people on this side will see what is happening on the other side and will say, My God! Pakistan "*ki tarf dekhna bhi nahi hai*" (don't even look towards Pakistan).'

K. Shankar Bajpai (Former Indian Ambassador to Pakistan, China and the US): I would like to draw our audience attention to one fact which is rather unfortunate: this session was supposed to be devoted to partnership between India and Pakistan for peace and prosperity but we have not been able to go beyond the Kashmir issue. I suppose that's what the Pakistani position has always been – that we cannot move to partnership without settlement of Kashmir.

May I suggest that there is no use trying to device formulae that might pass for solutions. We have to first try and change the circumstances. Dr Abdullah referred to the relationship between Germany and Britain. The more common example cited is between France and Germany which after centuries of bitter hatred were able to come to terms. Why? Because the circumstances changed and they were able to come to terms when faced by a common threat. Above all the leaderships in both countries realised that enough was enough. That has not happened in our case. You cannot solve Kashmir in today's circumstances but we can try and build up a relationship of cooperation and partnership in other areas which might one day permit a solution regarding Kashmir.

Q. Mr Imran Khan you have said that the decision of Jammu and Kashmir should be left to the people of Jammu and Kashmir. You are a Pakistani but the man who is sitting next to you is a Kashmiri. He has been elected thrice by the people of Jammu and Kashmir. You don't respect his view, so how can we expect Pakistan to respect the view of Jammu and Kashmir?

Imran Khan: If they are what are considered credible elections and Dr Abdullah then comes to power, we would respect his views. You know, I still respect his views but the problem right now is that who are the true representatives of Kashmir who will be recognised by everyone?

Altaf Hussain (Founder, MQM): I want to know the opinion of these leaders, their own opinion and not the opinion of their governments. First, do they want the areas which are with India to remain with India and the areas which are with Pakistan to remain with Pakistan? Second, should the LoC be considered a permanent border? And should there be an independent Kashmir?

Imran Khan: My position is very clear: it's the peoples' genuine representatives who should decide. If the people of Kashmir decide they want independence who am I to tell them that they must join us. That would make Kashmir a territorial rather than a rights issue.

Air Vice Marshall Kapil Kak (Retd.): Mr Imran Khan, you referred to the power of democracy even in a small country like Switzerland. What are the prospects of transition of Pakistan to democracy?

Imran Khan: I am a firm believer that there is no substitute to pure democracy. Having seen dictatorship and having also seen flawed democracy in Pakistan, I have come to the conclusion that no matter how bad democracy is, we must just keep giving it a chance.

India is a prime example. I envy the way the Indian elections were held. It's amazing that 350 million people turned out to vote; that a sitting government loses the election and that only three constituencies complain of some sort of inappropriateness.

I am an optimist. I believe there is a great transition happening at the grassroots level in Pakistan. The level of awareness in the country has increased tremendously, not just because we have had five elections in fifteen to sixteen years but also because independent television channels have sparked off this debate. In the last two years we've seen politicians on TV talking about everything, criticising the government. So, although we have been stuck a little bit, I have no doubt that it is matter of time before we have democracy.

Rajdeep Sardesai: But we also have a situation where you have one former prime minister who is in Jeddah, and another who flips between Dubai and London and your third largest party's leader can come to Delhi but not to Pakistan. Is it not a bit odd?

Imran Khan: I know the reason why one is in Jeddah and the other in Dubai but I do not know why Mr Altaf Hussain is in London.

Q. With regard to the election in Jammu and Kashmir in 2002 (incidentally, in the presence of all the major embassies of Delhi), do both panelists consider the Mufti government, as the elected government in Jammu and Kashmir, to be the true representative of Jammu and Kashmir?

Imran Khan: When I said true representative, I meant of the entire Kashmir region, bearing in mind that one-third of it is in Pakistan.

When Kashmir as a whole votes for its representatives it would be very different to the one that has been held now.

Rajdeep Sardesai: Farooq Abdullah would you accept that Mufti Mohammad Syed won a free and fair election?

Farooq Abdullah: He won fifteen seats and with fifteen seats he can't be a representative of Jammu and Kashmir. I had twenty-eight seats and I am not there because the Congress did not support us.

Rajdeep Sardesai: So, you chose the wrong coalition party.

Farooq Abdullah: It's not a question of coalition partners. I didn't have a coalition because I didn't want to form the government. I didn't want to have that *aaya Ram, gaya Ram* business. That's why I told my son not to form the government – though he regrets my decision now. But we would rather sit in the Opposition and fight it out.

Omar Abdullah: Mr Imran Khan was very profuse in his praise for the Indian election and how well they had done to remove Atal Behari Vajpayee's government and bring in the new UPA government. I am confused that if the Election Commission does such a good job in the rest of India, how come you are not willing to look at the same results for Jammu and Kashmir and suggest that these are free and fair as well?

Imran Khan: I answered that question before. The reason is that the election has to be held in the whole of Kashmir which includes the Pakistani side. Secondly, the area must be demilitarised. If you don't, there will always be doubts amongst outsiders that perhaps there the army did exert pressure or there was coercion.

Vinod Sharma (Senior Journalist): Mr Amanullah Khan has often said that there cannot be a solution on Kashmir unless that solution protects the respective national pride of India and Pakistan. Now, given the proposal which the National Conference makes about a soft border and given a certain degree of time for that to happen, can you have a solution by precedence, that is, you create precedence that becomes acceptable to people and one that respects the national pride of India and Pakistan?

Imran Khan: I am all for confidence-building measures. Dr Abdullah said the same thing. Anything that eases the tension is fine but there must be a roadmap. You cannot have confidence-building measures that just go on because from past experience we have seen that if the Kashmir dispute is left unattended, it will fester and people will take advantage of it.

We know that on both sides of the border there are people who would be willing to get votes by espousing hatred. If there is a roadmap, at least people will know which direction we are headed in.

Q. Abdullah, have the Kashmiris been given the fundamental right to political sovereignty? Have they been given the option to choose?

Farooq Abdullah: Well, I would ask the same question to you: have people in the Northern Territory or in Azad Kashmir and PoK been given the right to choose? I have met Sardar Ibrahim Khan a number of times in London he was also disgruntled about the entire situation.

The point is do we want to go forward? If you stick to your point then let me tell you that the roadmap is closed and there can be no forward movement. We must move forward in every other respect and Kashmir will automatically come into a solution as better relationships between two countries develop.

Rajdeep Sardesai: Imran Khan, if you had to go out and meet just one woman in India, who would that person be?

Imran Khan: I have just come out of a nine-year marriage. Give me some time!

Rajdeep Sardesai: Is there any one woman you have admired in India over these years?

Imran Khan: For us in the subcontinent, Sonia Gandhi's gesture (of turning down the prime ministership) is quite incredible. That someone would have the opportunity to become the prime minister and refuse and sit back and allow someone else to get the job is something that goes against the psyche of the subcontinent. I admired that a lot.

Rajdeep Sardesai: Farooq Abdullah, is there anyone that you want to meet in Pakistan?

Farooq Abdullah: I think you will have to give me permission

> The superpower status will have meaning and can be sustained only if the people of India are able to share in the process of growth. Growth must be inclusive. Growth must be all embracing. After providing what is absolutely essential and minimum for the people of India, only then we can really say that we have become an economic superpower.

Vision India

The Next Economic

Superpower

■

P. Chidambaram

■

P. Chidambaram

Union Minister for Finance

Scion of a prominent industrialist family from Chennai, Palaniappan Chidambaram chose to stay away from the predictable path of joining the family business and entered politics instead. This Harvard-educated lawyer first got elected to Parliament from the Sivaganga constituency in Tamil Nadu in 1984 and became a junior Interior Minister under Prime Minister Rajiv Gandhi.

Chidambaram was Rajiv's emissary to the Tamil Nadu leadership during the crisis of Sri Lankan Tamil refugees. After Rajiv was assassinated in 1991, Chidambaram was appointed Commerce Minister in the new government headed by P. V. Narasimha Rao. He fitted in well with the new pro-reforms lobby and his ministry was responsible for doing away with several red-tape regulations which boosted Indian exports.

Although he played a big part in writing the Congress manifesto in the 1996 elections, a disagreement with his party's decision over political alignments with J. Jayalalitha's All-India Anna Dravida Munnetra Kazhagam (AIADMK) led him to resign from the Congress and along with G.K. Moopanar set up a new political outfit – the Tamil Maanila Congress Democratic Front. He won his parliamentary seat with a handsome margin.

Chidambaram's return to the Congress party was inevitable once Sonia Gandhi took over the leadership. For many people, especially investors both domestic and foreign, His presence in the government is a positive signal. He is, after all, the architect of the much-acclaimed 'dream-budget' for 1996-97, in which he brought discipline in government spending and launched an ambitious tax reform programme.

A firm believer in free trade, Chidambaram is of the opinion that countries which are open to competitive societies have succeeded in removing poverty, while those which remain closed and controlled have not. He is also a strong supporter of the World Trade Organization and strongly believes that a rule-based global trading system will benefit developing countries.

MANY OF YOU ARE GATHERED HERE TO LISTEN, WITHOUT A TRACE OF CYNICISM OR DOUBT, TO SOMEONE SPEAK ON WHETHER INDIA CAN OR WILL be the next economic superpower. Had we attempted this thirteen years ago you might have scoffed at me and many of you would have left this room.

There is a belief that India can become the next superpower. In terms of gross national output we are already in the fourth position and within a decade and half we will displace Japan and take over the third position. But will that make India an economic superpower? I must, therefore, take a step back and ask myself and ask you to ask yourself: what is an economic superpower?

I think an economic superpower is a country which has a very large output and can match any other country in the production of goods and services. At the same time, the bulk of the people of that country must have a decent quality in standard of life. The BRICs report[1] and most commentators on India's status underscore India's capacity to raise its economic output.

Undoubtedly we will be there in the league of nations which are economic powerhouses. Already we have one of the world's largest and most efficient refineries. We are one of the world's largest optical media manufacturers. We have the world's largest laminated tube manufacturing capacity; and the world's largest capacity in denim. I could go on and on. Our capacity to produce goods and services is unquestionable.

In that sense we are perhaps knocking on the door of becoming a superpower. But a large number of people in India live in poverty. They have been deprived of drinking water, sanitation, electricity, basic medical care, schools, roads, and telephone connectivity. The per capita income is low; many are at the edge of deprivation and poverty. And, therefore, there is great doubt about aspiring to be a superpower.

1 Goldman Sachs, *Global Economics Paper No 99: Dreaming with BRICs: The Path to 2050* (October 2003).

Looking into the future, what do I see? I want to list these trends because I think these are important.

First look at the growth rates. Despite massive poverty in this country and low levels of investment, look at three periods of ten years each. Between 1972 and 1982, the average annual growth rate was 3.5 per cent. In the next ten years, between 1982 and 1992, it was 5.2 per cent. In the next twelve years between 1992 and 2004, it has so far been 6 per cent. It is possible, therefore, to raise the average annual growth rate to 7 per cent and, more perhaps closer to, 8 per cent in the next ten to twelve years.

Let us look at our engagement with the rest of the world. We attract far too little foreign investment and we import far too little. But our trade GDP ratio, which was 20 per cent, has increased to 35 per cent. Merchandising exports have grown 150 per cent and services exports have grown 275 per cent. Also we have a large population. Sometimes it does appear to be a burden and we must indeed moderate population growth, but look at the upside of this. Of the total population, 40 per cent is now a working population and this will rise to 50 per cent in 2020 and to 53 per cent in 2040.

Contrast this with other countries where the working population is declining. We will have a large number of people working – and working means earning, saving and with the savings going into investments.

What will happen to our children? Among the young today, 73 per cent are literate. It is still short of China which has 98 per cent literacy among the young. But what is heartening is that the ratio of expenditure on education to total expenditure in households has doubled in the eighties and nineties. Even the poor spend more on education. We will have in a few years a young population which is virtually 100 per cent literate.

What does this mean for the muscles and sinews that make for a superpower? It means that as the working population to total population increases, there will be higher savings rate and with the higher savings rate GDP growth will increase. With higher GDP growth, more households will be steadily pushed up the brackets where savings are positive. And as India becomes a more willing globaliser, more open to trade and investment, more foreign savings will flow into India. That, I believe, is the foundation for India's aspiration to becoming a superpower.

More savings and more investment by the Indian people, more foreign savings flowing into India, a larger proportion of people constituting the working population and with productivity increases which are visible – 2 per cent of our GDP is directly attributable to productivity increases – we can be absolutely certain in our mind that given good politics and good governance, we will maintain and sustain a growth rate of over 7 per cent, close to 8 per cent and indeed become an economic superpower.

But where will I find visible symbols of the superpower status? What do I want to find five years from today at the end of the term of this government? I would like to look back and say that we have left behind 30,000 km of world-class roads; six international airports of world-class stature, a dozen international world-class ports, all of India's children in the age group of five to ten in school; all of India's villages electrified – at least at the village level, if not at the household level; and all of India's villages connected by road. These are things that we should work for. While demography, aspirations of the people, good saving habits, globalization will work in India's favour to make India a superpower. Government and those who are in the government must turn their attention to people and what people need in order to be able to say that we have a decent life. We have a life of dignity. We have enough food. We have clean water. We have sanitation. We have roads. We have access to medical care.

You cannot be a superpower on the back of large number of people who are extremely poor. The superpower status will have meaning and can be sustained only if the people of India are able to share in the process of growth. Growth must be inclusive. Growth must be all embracing. After providing what is absolutely essential and minimum to the people of India, only then we can really say that we have become an economic superpower.

I do not want India to grow as a divided India with a part of India growing and becoming a part of the developed world and another part of India struggling and languishing in poverty. That is unsustainable. That is unacceptable. And that has to be rejected. While we grow, and we can grow and we have proved how we can grow, we must ensure that all of India marches with us on this journey towards the status of being an economic superpower.

Moderator | **Ashok Desai**

Former Chief Economic Consultant,
Ministry of Finance

Ashok Desai: You said that our growth rate in the last ten years was 6 per cent and then you said that in the next ten to twelve years we might raise it to 7 or maybe 8 per cent. East Asian countries have grown consistently at 9 per cent to 10 per cent. Our last Prime Minister used to talk about 10 per cent growth and you have talked about 7 to 8 per cent growth. Is it possible that you are being truly modest and that you are really in the business of redistributing poverty rather than growth?

P. Chidambaram: Growth does not happen in a vacuum. Growth is crucially dependent upon the level of savings, the level of investment and the incremental output ratio. If 26 per cent of India is extremely poor, it is foolhardy to promise growth of 10 per cent. Even to grow at over 7 per cent or close to 8 per cent, our investment to GDP must rise to close to 30 per cent. Therefore, I don't take umbrage at being described as modest and accept that we have modest abilities compared to those of some others.

I am realistic and I want to build this huge nation brick by brick. As more and more people join the working population, more and more people will move up the ladder. There will be more and more savings and there will be more and more investments. At the same time, more and more foreign investment will flow in. But it will not happen overnight. It will happen over a period of five to ten years. Therefore, I would like to sustain growth at 7 per cent close to 8 per cent, and then move up hopefully, if there is good governance and good politics. Irrespective of the party in power we can reach the 10 per cent growth rate by the end of this decade.

M.E. Nkoana Mashabane (High Commissioner, South Africa): I am wondering whether India is taking full advantage of all the opportunities

that are there in the neighbourhood and in the countries and regions around the Indian Ocean rim? Are you, for example, taking full advantage of the partnership with Africa as a continent? What is the possibility of looking at strengthening security partnerships and keeping the Indian Ocean rim as a zone of peace?

P. Chidambaram: I agree that we are not as fully engaged with Africa as we should be. But let me say, with a measure of regret, that it is not intentions that lead to engagement but opportunity; opportunity for trade and investment and that alone will lead to engagement. Private business and, even now, public sector business cannot be easily directed by ministries or ministers to engage a country or region.

I see opportunities opening for us in the US, in Europe and, increasingly, in Southeast Asia and the Far East. It appears that we will have opportunities in the Commonwealth of Independent States, in West Asia or in the Middle East. We would have had opportunities in East Africa but my experience over the last ten to twelve years is that these opportunities that we thought were there were not? My approach is that we should actively look for opportunities for trade and investment and if we can maximise these, you will find the engagement with Africa is deeper. Otherwise we will continue to meet and exchange polite conversation. Hard engagement can only come if we can trade more with each other and we can invest more in each other's countries.

Manzar Khan (Sports Management Group International, London): You have talked of good signs of an economic superpower – sanitation, healthcare and so on. But what are the policies to make the development in these areas sustainable? Do you have any policy or structure in place where you are going to involve people from the grassroots level?

P. Chidambaram: I coined the phrase 'cooperative federalism' seven or eight years ago and we are, both the previous government and my government, engaged in building consensus among states for tax reform. Now that the states are on board, I think we need to do the same thing in other areas such as agriculture, education and roads. I think we should get away from central government/state governments where I provide funds and you are accountable to me. I think it is possible to build consensus by involving state governments in India.

In the region, I am afraid we have very different degrees of closeness in our relationships. We have reasonably good relations, economic relations, with Sri Lanka and Nepal. With Bangladesh we have had our good and bad times. With Pakistan we are still struggling to establish a relationship based on MFN (most favoured nation). I can't really say that either this government or the previous government and the one before that has been able to make much headway as far as regional cooperation is concerned. SAARC is there but it is easier to forge a Free Trade Agreement (FTA) with Thailand, it is easier to negotiate a FTA with Singapore, ASEAN than get SAFTA off the ground which is a pity. While geography determines our future, history seems to be a big burden on us. But our engagement with Southeast Asia is deepening and if the FTAs and the economic cooperation agreements that are under negotiation come through, as I believe they will over the next six months to a year, you will find that in the region we become a very active player.

Q. Finance Minister you have talked about the growth rates and the incremental investment rates. You have talked about how the demography of this country is changing and many more people are joining the work force. But I think the government must also adopt a proactive solution in terms of the rupee raise and savings in investment. What are your thoughts on this? On the other issue of health, sanitation and education, I think the issue isn't one of funding but of implementation and accountability.

P. Chidambaram: On the first question, our growth rates have more or less stagnated over the last five or six years – they go up a per cent and come down a per cent. Experience and figures show that as people move up the economic ladder they tend to save more. The poor save but they don't have enough to save, therefore they don't save enough. But as people move up, saving rates go up to as high as 36 per cent. The answer then is to create more jobs and create more high-income jobs to make savings rise.

I have often said that India is able to keep its head above water because our parents save. The public sector neither saves nor dis-saves. The private sector is a marginal saver. The government sectors are notorious dis-savers. The only ones who save in this country are households. Therefore, if tax rates can be moderated and more people brought into the tax net, leaving more money with people who save, I think the savings rate will go up as incomes go up.

The second question is one that all governments have wrestled with for the last twenty years. I am convinced in my mind that the system of state and central governments delivering electricity or roads or water or sanitation has simply failed in this country and will continue to fail if we put our faith in central and state government servants.

We must trust communities and give ownership to the community. The *panchayat* is the representative group of the community and the *panchayat* I believe must own, not in the legal sense, but own the school, the hospital, the primary healthcare centre, the road, the water body in the village, the village tank, the village electricity distribution system must all be 'owned' by the community. Unless you are willing to trust your village *panchayats* and your *panchayat samitis* with ownership of these assets and functions, you cannot deliver what has to be delivered to 600,000 villages.

This is one of the reasons why Rajiv Gandhi campaigned throughout the length and breath of this country to introduce *Panchayati Raj*. The Act was passed after he passed away and has been implemented by people who had no heart or soul in it. Today I think there is a minister who is deeply committed to implementing *Panchayati Raj* but all other ministers must join in. All other ministries must join as well. Ultimately ownership of these assets, ownership of these functions must be with village communities or the *panchayats*.

Q. The recently concluded US Presidential election reflects some important uncertainties. First there is increased uncertainty in energy security and the availability of affordable energy. Second, there could be volatility both in the management of the exchange rate and the management of interstate policy. How is India going to respond?

P. Chidambaram: I am not so pessimistic about the energy situation because I think the US build inventories in the run up to the election. I thought it was a closely guarded secret but I think some figures have come out that perhaps we will continue to face high crude oil prices through November, December and January but once the winter is over, I think these inventories are unsustainable and must be liquidated.

There is still a surplus of supply over demand and I think oil prices will moderate after January. If they don't then we have to live with these energy prices. Our decision to raise fuel prices was a very difficult step taken after three months and after two price rises by this government. But I do hope people will understand. These are not matters within our control.

On the second issue, I don't think there is anyone in the world who understands the enigmatic Mr Alan Greenspan. But please remember that we have to ensure that growth is not stifled while exchange rate adjustments continue to be made and monetary policy continues to be fine-tuned by the Reserve Bank of India. I must also plead the case for growth and it cannot be stifled or stunted or killed. This country needs growth and for it, we need a benign interest rate regime. We need adequate credit and liquidity. But these are issues which don't have an answer. I mean I could give you an answer today that could change dramatically a few days later.

So, our approach is that while we must have a very carefully calibrated monetary policy, we must ensure that growth is not stifled. Growth is an imperative not a luxury for India – a 7 or 8 per cent growth is an imperative for India.

Scott Bayman (President & CEO, GE-India): You talked about your goals on infrastructure. My question is how much is this going to cost and where will the funding come from? We have talked a little bit about savings being insufficient so it was suggested that you either turn to foreign direct investment (FDI) or go with public sector disinvestments to fund some of this infrastructure, which may be difficult in light of your coalition partners.

P. Chidambaram: All of it will play a part. I expect more people to comply with tax laws. I am sure everyone in this audience, every Indian citizen, has paid his taxes by the 31st of October. As more people comply with the tax laws, the tax revenue will show greater buoyancy. Public sector disinvestments are not ruled out. We are now facing a backlash against the policy pursued in the last three-four years. I am not being judgmental. I am just making a statement of fact. So we have to now reconstruct that policy and put in its place one that is acceptable to the people and to our coalition partners.

Every poll has shown that over 60 per cent of India is opposed to mindless disinvestment. Now without being judgmental, I have to take note of that sentiment. Therefore, the public sector disinvestment policy will have to be reworked and reinvented and put in place so that our coalition partners, Parliament and people accept that policy. Once we have in place an acceptable policy, public sector disinvestment will also give revenues.

The third, of course, is foreign direct investment. Again we will have to put in place a policy that is acceptable to our coalition, to my friends in the Opposition and to the people at large.

I sincerely hope that people will not change their positions. It is easy to deal with fixed positions, more difficult to deal with changing positions. I sincerely hope that we will be able to arrive at a consensus on FDI and if we arrive at a consensus, I think more FDIs will flow into India.

I am not saying this basket is more important than that basket or that basket is more important than the third basket. But please remember 98 per cent of all of India's investible resources are Indian resources. Today we have companies which are confident that they can go abroad and raise money: Reliance, Tata, Bharti, National Thermal Power Cooperation. State Bank is going abroad to raise money. I don't have a dearth of capital. What I have a dearth of are bankable projects. I need bankable projects and the people who can implement them on time.

India in the Twenty-first Century

The NDA Vision

Superpower

■

Arun Jaitley

■

Arun Shourie

■

Suresh Prabhakar Prabhu

■

Moderator

Barkha Dutt

Senior Editor, NDTV

Arun Jaitley

Senior BJP Leader & Former Union Minister

Arun Jaitley, the former Union Minister of Law and Justice and Commerce and Industry, was first appointed Minister of State for Information and Broadcasting (independent charge) in October 1999. He was also appointed Minister of State for Disinvestment, a new ministry created to give effect to the policy of disinvestments under the World Trade Organization (WTO) regime. He took over the additional charge of the Ministry of Law, Justice and Company Affairs on 23 July 2000.

Jaitley was elevated as the Cabinet Minister in November 2000 and was made simultaneously the Minister of Law, Justice and Company Affairs and Shipping. He was the first Minister of Shipping following the bifurcation of the Ministry of Surface Transport. He subsequently demitted the office of the Minister for Shipping and Minister of Law, Justice and Company Affairs to become Secretary General of the Bharatiya Janata Party as its national spokesperson.

Born on 28 December 1952, Jaitley graduated in commerce from the Sri Ram College of Commerce, New Delhi, and passed his law exam from the Faculty of Law, University of Delhi in 1977. A distinguished student, Jaitley was President of the Delhi University Students Union and, during the Emergency, was jailed for nineteen months. Jaitley was a prominent member of the movement against corruption launched by Jai Prakash Narayan.

Acknowledged as one of the brightest lawyers of his generation, Jaitley has been practising law since 1977 and is a designated senior advocate. In 1990 he was appointed Additional Solicitor General of India.

He was a delegate of the Government of India to the United Nations General Assembly Session in June 1998 where the Declaration on Law relating to Drugs and Money Laundering was approved. He led the Indian delegation at several trade dialogues including at Cancun.

Jaitley is married with two children.

Arun Shourie

Senior BJP Leader & Former Union Minister

Arun Shourie is a well-known author and was the editor of a leading newspaper before he was elected to the Rajya Sabha as a candidate of the Bharatiya Janata Party in 1998. Born on 2 November 1941, in Jalandhar, he completed his schooling from Modern School, New Delhi. He has a PhD in economics from St Stephen's College, Delhi, and from the University of Syracuse, USA.

Shourie has received several national and international awards including the Padma Bhushan, Magsaysay Award, Dadabhai Naoroji Award, Astor Award and International Editor of the Year Award. He is acclaimed as one of 'World Press Freedom Heroes' by the International Press Institute, a 'Star of Asia' by *Business Week* and 'Business Leader of the Year' by the Economic Times jury.

In November 1999, he was appointed Minister of State in the Ministry of Statistics and Programme Implementation, a position he held until 31 August 2001. He has also been a Minister of State in the Department of Administrative Reforms and Public Grievances of the Ministry of Personnel, Public Grievances and Pensions and Minister of State (independent charge) of the Department of Disinvestment. He was made Minister of Commerce and Industry and has also held the post of Minister of Communications and Information Technology.

Shourie's recent book, *Courts and their Judgments*, looks at the way India's law courts have extended their roles, because of the shortcomings of other Indian institutions. He has also written books that examine the internal processes of the government.

Shourie has published seventeen books and is highly regarded for his incisive comments on the way Indian systems function. He continues to write as a columnist for various publications.

He is married to Anita Shourie and has one son.

Suresh Prabhakar Prabhu

Shiv Sena Leader & Former Union Minister

Suresh Prabhakar Prabhu was born on 11 July 1953 in Bombay (now Mumbai). He graduated in commerce from Bombay University and obtained a law degree from the same university. He has also passed the F.C.A. from the Institute of Chartered Accountants, New Delhi.

Prabhu was elected to the eleventh Lok Sabha in 1996. Prior to this he was the chairman of the Maharashtra State Finance Commission (from 1995 to 1996). In 1998 he was re-elected to the twelfth Lok Sabha and was appointed Union Cabinet Minister of Industry. He has also headed the Ministry of Environment and Forests and has been a Cabinet Minister for Chemicals and Fertilizers.

Prabhu has published papers on a variety of subjects including economics, sociology and taxation. He is the Chairman of the Konkan Kala Academy and Vice-chairman, of the All India Central apex body of Marathi stage.

Prabhu is connected with a large number of organisations working in the fields of education, literary activities, sports, adult education, mentally-retarded children, hospital, theatre and drama. He is also associated with trade associations like the World Chamber of Commerce and Industry. He is a former Chairman of the Saraswat Co-operative Bank.

Prabhu continues to serve on the board of directors of several companies and has been in the executive committee for International voluntary service in Paris. He is an active participant in sports, arts, the literary and music world and is considered a leading chartered accountant.

Prabhu is married to Uma and has a son.

BARKHA DUTT: L. K. ADVANI TOOK OVER AS PRESIDENT OF THE BJP, HE WAS ASKED WHETHER HINDUTVA WOULD CONTINUE TO BE A POLITICAL MANTRA FOR HIS PARTY. HE CLARIFIED THAT it might not be Hindutva but nationalism.

We've had some NDA allies since then, with perhaps an eye on the Bihar elections, talking about the dangers of BJP returning to hard Hindutva. For the past four years we've been debating the distinction between hard and soft Hindutva. In recent times, the big question has been, what went wrong for the NDA? How is the NDA going to reinvent itself? How is the BJP going to reinvent itself? Has Hindutva become an anachronism, at least as an electoral issue?

Arun Jaitley: As far as electoral issues are concerned, I think one of the worrisome issues which has been confronting us over the last fifteen years and now seems to be increasingly coming to the forefront, is that ideological issues are taking a backseat. Issues of governance have also taken a backseat.

If you were, for instance, to analyse the results of the last Parliamentary election, one of the most startling features has been, that though it was a national election it became an aggregate of state polls with each state voting on the basis of factors within that state. Even adjacent states – Punjab and Haryana, Andhra Pradesh and Karnataka, Tamil Nadu and Kerala – voted in dramatically different directions.

Everything boiled down to the kind of election alliances and the social combination you had and that is a worrisome factor. So, the answer to your question on whether Hindutva has become a non-electable factor is that, it could be so in Chattisgarh and Madhya Pradesh, but not in, say, Bihar.

The question of alliances and electable factors is a little different. The ideological factor is also different. If you had a connection between governance and electibility, I can assure you that the ruling alliance in Maharashtra would not have been voted back to power; you would not have the same government for the past fourteen years in Bihar. Elections in India depend on a host of other factors, not necessarily the governance factor or the ideological factor.

However, the nationalist ideology in India – and that would extend beyond merely the political factors – particularly in the context in which we are placed would continue to have extreme relevance. Amongst the major challenges confronting us, we have economic challenges and the challenge to fight poverty but one of the most important factors would be the threat to sovereignty.

For instance – and it is not only in the context of Jammu and Kashmir or the Northeast or terrorism – it is also relevant in the emerging Maoist corridor across the centre of the country right from Nepal downwards. Therefore these issues, irrespective of the words we use, whether nationalism or Hindutva which Mr Advani used almost interchangeably, would remain of extreme relevance.

Governance alone won't win you the election unless politics, alliances, social bases, keeping your constituencies

Barkha Dutt: It is interesting what you say about ideology taking a back seat in India's political future because ideology is what once distinguished the BJP from other parties. What is the BJP's distinctive political identity going to be?

Arun Shourie: Actually it is Arun Jaitley who will speak for the BJP. Prabhu will speak for the NDA. I can only speak for myself.

Barkha Dutt: I take that point. But I imagine the political affiliations are largely on the same side still.

Arun Shourie: I am sure you are right on that. But if the question is narrowed down like this it will not be of much interest even to you. If you were truly thinking of secularism and communalism and so on, we would object to the fact that the essence of secularism, or of a non-BJP ideology as you call it, is that the individual should be the unit of state policy and not a group.

The evolution of European political thought and of every other country is that we will never concede to a religious group what we will not concede to a secular group or that we will never concede to one religious group what we will deny to another religious group. Any differences on this? No. But what do we do in reservations which are not being extended on the basis of religion? We are talking only of the group as a basis of state policy not the individual. Similarly, this whole demand, when we say we never concede to one religious group, but you will deny to another. You should never concede to a religious group but you will deny to a secular group.

You see what happens to institutions, which are called minority institutions, under Article 29. How they must be given state aid. But you cannot interfere or take even a step which would ensure better administration of those institutions. Minority institutions are not confined to running courses which are germane to the culture of the minority. It could be anything as long as the board or the founder-members of the board are a majority of the minority

you are able to blend it with some kind of prudent intact. – Arun Jaitley

community. So you could have two engineering colleges in Hyderabad. The one across the road is a minority institution. Both have to be given state aid. But in one case you cannot even take a step towards improving its administration. You cannot take a step to do something about capitation fees or other similar issues. If I write about it, am I communal or is this Hindutva or what? There is a disease in Indian public discourse that every issue is now to be seen whether it is Hindutva or non-Hindutva.

I can give you half a dozen official reports which have said that India is losing territory – this is the word, territory is being annexed by people from Bangladesh. They happened to be of one religion. If I write about this, it is Hindutva. So, I believe that the way you frame the question itself shows the extent to which the discourse and, therefore, public policy has got perverse. The problem that results because of this is that each political group is unable to go to the electorate on the basis of performance and so, goes and appeals to various sections. Since Mr Gandhi's time what we do is to frighten a section of people and then present ourselves as the only available saviour. This happens with caste, with minorities and we now have a completely splintered electorate leading to splintered legislatures with forty-three parties in the Lower House.

It is not a question of Hindutva, it is a much more fundamental question to which we should at some stage come to talk about remedies.

Barkha Dutt: Taking the debate beyond what you, Mr Shourie, believe a certain kind of perverse over-simplification, the question still remains: what went wrong for the National Democratic Alliance (NDA)? Is there an assessment? Suresh Prabhu, the Shiv Sena is considered perhaps more right wing than the BJP. What do you believe went wrong for you in Maharashtra?

Suresh Prabhu: I think the audience would be interested in talking more about India than about Maharashtra.

Barkha Dutt: But looking back to look ahead.

Suresh Prabhu: Let's look a little at the broader picture, at what went wrong for the NDA. You would like to know the answer in terms of the elections. But an election could be lost and that is a temporary phenomenon. I completely agree with what Arun Jaitley has said that the election was an aggregate of state elections. It was, really speaking, a municipal election where people voted for local issues rather than for a national election. Unfortunately, therefore, the NDA could not project the real one single national issue around which people could vote. If you go state by state and analyse the results, with the exception of Bihar and West Bengal, in each of the states, voters actually voted against their state governments for the national election. That is how it really went on.

But also we could not project what we did in the right perspective. What we said was that India is shining. Had we said that we have done quite a lot in six years – and you can compare those six years with any other six-year period or even the preceding forty-four years. This particular government did quite a lot from roads, telephone connections, reforms in the power sector to initiatives in the water sector.

But what we actually projected was that India is shining. We have done so much. This made it very easy for the Opposition to ask the people, 'Is your life shining?' India is such a vast country of one billion people with more than 6 per cent out of the poverty line and 28 per cent below it. If you go by the statistics of people who actually earn less than $1 a day that is more; if you take people who earn less than $2 a day that is still more. We just could not communicate to the people what we meant when we said India is shining. We could not communicate to them that India has changed, that we have done a lot of things.

Any election is actually the management of expectations. If you raise expectations so high while in government or when you come to power and then go in for an election, people compare their expectations with what they have got. The important thing is how can we continue on the path of sustained growth. For the first time India had a vision document. What it will be like by 2020, for example? This must be a shared vision, shared by all the people in the country including all political parties.

Barkha Dutt: Does that vision of the NDA remain unchanged? There has been a change in leadership within the party and there is a new team in place. There is a lot of public and internal party debate. Has that vision altered?

Arun Jaitley: I don't think there has been a change nor is there likely to be one, whether it's the NDA vision or the BJP vision. In fact, I have one of the vision documents which we prepared at the time of elections right in front of me. There is very little difference between the two documents, between the parties and the NDA and I do believe that in the six years of governance as far as the NDA is concerned, we attempted, to the best of our ability, proper and good governance.

We had an agenda where economic decision making was far easier than what it is today. Mr Shourie had to be party to some of the most difficult decisions in the government, but ultimately he found that the eventual centre of power usually sided with him even in radical decisions.

Today the process of decision making – economic decision making – in the country is far different, far slower, than what it was.

The concentration on infrastructure, on making Indian industry both in the services and also manufacturing sector globally more competitive, the kind of difficult steps required to be taken in that direction were all part of the NDA performance. There is no dilution or rethinking as far as this agenda is concerned.

If we were to sum up three reasons why we lost the elections, I don't think we lost because we unleashed Indian energies in the economic area or because of governance. The first reason is that the election, as I mentioned earlier, was an aggregate of state polls and in some crucial states, our alliances did not do well. Our caste, or social combination as we prefer to call it these days, was not effective enough and there is no conflict between that and the governance agenda. We have to try to correct the error.

The second reason, which is little more disturbing is that it was not

There is a disease in Indian public discourse that every non-Hindutva.

just the NDA but also Chandrababu Naidu in Andhra Pradesh. Why did S.M. Krishna lose Karnataka? It appears that positive electoral campaigns on the basis of performance in a developing economy like ours have inherently become more difficult.

The third reason, was the realisation that in the process of concentrating on governance and even during the elections, we perhaps ignored our constituency.

Barkha Dutt: Which constituency would that be?

Arun Jaitley: For any political party, its cadres and its support bases are its constituency. Its ideological supporters are its constituency and its social base is its constituency. The social base may be accrued to you for a number of reasons. But the conclusion is that if you are going in for electoral success, don't bank exclusively on governance. Blend it with some kind of prudent politics. Governance alone won't win you the election unless you are able to blend it with some kind of prudent politics, alliances, social bases, keeping your constituencies intact.

Barkha Dutt: Mr Shourie I know you speak only on behalf of yourself and not on behalf of the BJP or Shiv Sena. Would you say that one of the things that the NDA got wrong was the assessment of the mood of the country with regard to Sonia Gandhi who many believe led the Congress to victory? Therefore, if Hindutva is, as you believe, a non-starter for a political debate, was the foreign origin issue a non-starter as well?

Arun Shourie: I think journalists have become a bit like psephologists and a bit like astrologers.

Barkha Dutt: Because we get it wrong?

Arun Shourie: Not that we get it wrong but that we are so quick with explanations *after* we have got it wrong. That, of course includes me as a journalist. The moment something happens we have fifty-three explanations instantly on television. Often in cabinet, there would

issue is now to be seen whether it is Hindutva or
– Arun Shourie

be people who would say, '*Nahin sahib, is sey yeh signal kharaab ho jayega. Nahin sahi, yeh constituency offend ho jayegi*. (Oh no, if we do this, people will get the wrong signals or our constituency will be offended).' Atalji would say, '*Dekhiye sarkarein aateen hain or jaati hain* (Governments come and go) but we have a duty towards the country.'

This sense of obligation, of duty towards the country, I don't know how it works today in many of the decisions that are being taken and in many of these competitive populist promises which are being made, such as those made in Andhra Pradesh for which the state is now going to pay. Or, in Maharashtra.

These were things which Mr Vajpayee foreclosed at the threshold itself. I think there is one other feature in what you are saying about the vision and the way in which it now differs. Many of the things that we see affecting national security today are things which fill me with great foreboding. That is the defining difference between this coalition and the coalition led by a person like Mr Vajpayee. The fact that people who are out to break the country, whose declared objective is to make this corridor between Nepal and Andhra Pradesh and between Gujarat and Orissa should be allowed to roam around with their guns on the pretext of a ceasefire.

There are ominous reports that have not been published, but are accounts given to the highest people of the way in which a declaration was agreed to in New York for which we will have to pay dearly in the future. In the NDA government, in Mr Vajpayee's time, the way Manipur has been allowed to fester would just never have been allowed.

Similarly, I heard from my friends in Andhra Pradesh that assistance was taken of groups committed to violence (during the elections) and that the price for that support will have to be paid very

We just could not communicate to the people what we to them that India has changed.

soon. The laxity with which ULFA has been treated in Assam ever since Mr Gogoi has come to power and now, what we are seeing in Andhra Pradesh with regard to the Naxalites are prices that are being paid.

You say 'India Shining' is a phrase. The fact of the matter is that India was and is shining. Just see the splendid way in which our services have grown; the splendid way in which young talent, yourself, all your colleagues, every new profession has opened up and been filled by very talented people. Channels, product design, information technology – professions which you have not heard of, fashion designing – any fashion that comes up and you have a rush of talent and world-class excellence and new manufacturing.

Barkha Dutt: My question might seem over simplified, according to Mr Shourie, but it is a question that many people in this country are asking: did the NDA get Sonia Gandhi's hold over this country wrong? I come back with the same question.

Arun Jaitley: Since you have pointedly asked the question again, you deserve an answer and my answer very simply is that certainly the president of a political party which emerges as the largest in Parliament does get credit for keeping his or her party together and, therefore, leading that party to an electoral verdict.

But some television people also have a habit of overstating the role of individuals in elections. We recently had the Maharashtra elections. Since 1952, the results showed that the Congress got the lowest ever number of seats and yet, I saw a number of television anchors giving credit to an individual for the great success of the party. I remember when Mr Sitaram Kesri led the Congress to 144 seats in Parliament he was almost physically thrown out of the Working Committee. Exactly at 144 seats this time, you are accusing

meant by India is shining. We could not communicate
– Suresh Prabhakar Prabhu

us of misjudging the mood of the country. Individuals have an important role but let us not understate or overstate that role.

Barkha Dutt: And let's remember that the NDA also fought an election in Mr Vajpayee's name and that he was the prime selling point of the campaign. The populist decisions by the Andhra Pradesh government, the fact is that in Maharashtra an issue like free electricity was something promised by both political formations, the BJP-Sena and the Congress-NCP. Looking at the economic model and taking the example of free electricity, what is the defining difference between the economic vision of the NDA and the Congress?

Suresh Prabhu: When I was the power minister, all state governments started charging minimum rates for bonds. We passed a law in Parliament which still exists, that any state government that would like to give free electricity must provide for it from its own budget. So, there is a fundamental difference between free electricity that was given earlier and free electricity that can now be given. If tariffs are not going to be charged, the state government must provide for that amount in its budget. And if it fails to provide it then the actual tariff as stipulated by the regulator applies.

There are state governments like Andhra Pradesh where there was an opinion that farmers were being forced to commit suicide as input costs were increasing – and one of the major input costs in the farm sector is electricity – and that should be billed. You have to balance populism with being more humane.

Barkha Dutt: Are you in favour of free electricity for farmers?

Suresh Prabhu: There is a saying in Marathi that you can't donate at somebody else's expense. You have to do it at your own cost. So, if I have to be generous, I must make provisions in my own budget. State electricity boards that were carrying the burden of such freebies are no longer responsible. It must be provided by the state government.

Moderator | **Barkha Dutt**

Senior Editor, NDTV

Venkatnarayan (Senior Journalist): Mr Arun Jaitley, the manner in which the BJP conducted itself in the last election and the way the MPs of your party behaved in Parliament gives one the impression that you had a problem believing you are actually out of power and that the Congress was in. As a result, instead of being a constructive Opposition you have tended to be a destructive Opposition. Are you now reconciled to being in the Opposition and what kind of behaviour could one look forward to in the next session of Parliament?

Arun Jaitley: The issue of Parliament is something that concerned the entire country and I can assure you we ourselves have been concerned and worried about it. A Parliamentary stalemate is not necessarily a happy occasion. A Parliamentary stalemate or even Parliamentary obstructionism is perhaps the last of Parliamentary tactics within the Parliament framework available to us.

I say this with a sense of regret that if the space meant for opposition is denied to an Opposition in Parliament then and only then is this last weapon resorted to. I am sure you will not deny that there were several issues which were raised in the last session of Parliament on which a debate was needed; a statement at the highest level or an explanation at the highest level was needed. For the first time in this country you had a very large, not criminalisation of politics, but criminalisation of the council of ministers.

If the prime ministerial prerogative of whom to induct is utilised in this manner, then Parliament is entitled to an explanation from the prime minister himself. Now, if the entire space is denied to the Opposition and, on the other hand, you have a resolution moved in one of the Houses condemning the Opposition, then this is not the way in which a government or treasury bench conducts Parliament. You have to give the Opposition the space which is entitled to it in Parliament. But if you squeeze the Opposition, you invite Parliamentary obstructionism, however unfortunate that might be.

D. Raja (Secretary, Communist Party of India): You have been saying that ideology has taken a backseat. Yet sometime back Mr Advani went on record to say we are not apologetic as far as Hindutva is concerned. Now you are trying to use different phrases – Hindutva, Bharatiyata or nationalism, whatever you may say – yet you have an ideological position: you consider the Left your number one ideological enemy. After all we are a democracy and in a democracy we should respect the verdict of the people.

In the last elections people gave their verdict against communal politics, whatever you may call it, and also against the new, liberal economic policies that explains why Mr Chandrababu Naidu and Mr S.M. Krishna were defeated. I am not able to understand why you cannot reconcile to the situation in which you stand defeated and why you don't want to honour the verdict of the people. That is why you are talking about 'aggregate of state elections'. What do you mean? Even in the 'aggregate of state elections', you did not get the numbers. Why can't you honour the peoples' verdict? Why can't you respect democracy? Do you have a concept of democracy?

Arun Shourie: There are those on the Left who talk insistently about ideology. Please look at their practice in West Bengal. In matters like economic policy, the choices are not as wide as they are made out to be to some participants in public. If I may say so, in spite of the Left being with the new government, Dr Manmohan Singh, Mr Chidambaram, when you hear them in New York are they not speaking on behalf of India and of the government?

Please look at the practice in West Bengal. Secondly, the economic policies being followed by the government itself. It is not a question of ideology not being important. In fact in India the discourse on ideology has been reduced to such perversity it seems that types of ideologies are not important as far as reconciling oneself to it. So that now that we are in the Opposition, we continue to behave exactly like the Opposition of the past that is exactly what the Congress used to do.

We have been in power for six years and more than fifty years in the Opposition. We have adequate experience of reconciling ourselves to that position. The problem is that my friends in the Left have not reconciled to their real position, that they want to keep this government in power, to support this government on the floor of the House and yet want to continue to occupy the Opposition space.

Mr Advani has said be proud of your ideology. We are. But he also repeatedly said that ideology takes a backseat when it comes to governance. The best example of this is not really the NDA government or now the Congress or the UPA government at the Centre, but the West Bengal government under the present Chief Minister. I find very little of what would be your traditional ideological moorings in the functioning of that government because in governance even he seems to have realised that the options are narrowing and even your government will have to move as per those narrowed options.

Jyotiraditya Scindia (Member of Parliament, Congress): My question is for Mr Shourie or Mr Jaitley. As you mentioned in your opening remarks there is not much difference between the agenda of the BJP and the members of the NDA coalition. I would like your response specifically on the issue of the Ram Temple.

Arun Jaitley: We in the BJP originally believed that there are three methodologies of resolving the issue. The first was legislation and we ourselves realised that in the absence of a broader Parliamentary consensus, such a solution was a little more difficult. We, therefore, go back to the two other options: try and resolve it by a process of negotiation and, if that does not work, take the second resort – a judicial process. This is a categorical statement in the NDA agenda and also a part of what the BJP documents have stated. In fact Mr George Fernandes and Mr Advani broadly converge on this view and we are again meeting to make sure there is no confusion in this regard within the NDA.

Arun Shourie: You know the Ramjanmabhoomi movement was in my view one of the defining moments in the correction of pseudo secularism and the contribution it made in raising a debate on many issues on which people like me wrote at that time. If pandering to sections is revived again, as is happening in Andhra Pradesh and other places, you will see a much stronger movement, whatever anybody may say.

N.K. Singh (Member, Planning Commission): Mr Arun Jaitley, if you look back at the six-year period of your government, what, would you believe, were the two key missed economic opportunities?

Arun Jaitley: Before I pointedly come to any illustrations, I would like to list the great achievement of the NDA government was to institutionalise and hasten the decision-making process as far as the economy was concerned.

There were areas of difficulty because of coalition politics; there were areas of difficulty because of lack of understanding on a large number of issues. For instance, globalisation was blamed for farmer suicides in Andhra Pradesh whereas India has been reasonably and rightly providing protection in agriculture. So, the answer really has to be on the terms of policy domain. I wish that the area that my friend Suresh Prabhu was subsequently looking at, namely, the interlinking of rivers, instead of starting in the third or fourth year of the six-year tenure had really started in the first or the second year, so that just like the national highways and rural roads, we could have actually put the implementation of this somewhere on track and that the subsequent government instead of saying we are going to review this went ahead with it because water is one of the core problems as far as rural India is concerned.

Second, the process of power sector reforms which Suresh started again and which we started implementing because really the onus of implementation had to be on the states, could have been much faster with the cooperation of the states themselves.

Barkha Dutt: Is there any Congress or Opposition chief minister whose work you admire or endorse?

Arun Shourie: Mr Buddhadev Bhattacharya. I seriously mean it because I visited West Bengal quite frequently at that time and was most impressed by his dedication to turning things around. He realised the cost of what had happened, he wanted very much to move forward and I remember the new work that was being done beyond Salt Lake City and making a new, future Kolkata was wonderful.

Secondly, in the Northeast I came across the work of Mr Sarkar in Tripura. It was exemplary work and it also happened to be a CPM government. I was equally surprised at the loss by Mr S.M. Krishna. I felt that in many ways, he too, like Chandrababu Naidu was trying to steer his people to look at the future. He was helped in this by industry, by modern people, but he was a person who was really doing this very well.

SAARC has the potential of unifying South Asia and converting it into an economic powerhouse in the global world economy.

Unity and Diversity

Keeping South Asia

Together

■

Chandrika Bandaranaike Kumaratunga

■

Chandrika Bandaranaike Kumaratunga

President, Sri Lanka

Chandrika Bandaranaike Kumaratunga, President of Sri Lanka for the past ten years, has had an unusual political and personal life. She is the daughter of Sirimavo Bandaranaike, who in 1960, became the world's first woman Prime Minister. Chandrika is, in fact, one of the very few world leaders both of whose parents have been heads of government. Her father, S.W.R.D. Bandaranaike, was the Prime Minister from 1956 to 1959.

Perhaps no other South Asian leader has suffered greater personal loss as a result of terrorism than Chandrika. Her husband, actor-politician Vijaya Kumaratunga, was assassinated in 1988. Her father, S.W.R.D. Bandaranaike, was shot dead in 1959 when Chandrika was just fourteen. She herself narrowly escaped death in 1999 when targeted by a suicide bomber, but lost an eye in the blast.

Born on 29 June 1945, Chandrika became a radical Leftist in the 1960s while studying political science in Paris and, on her return home, plunged headlong into land reform and youth action.

Her party, People's Alliance, came to power on 19 August 1994 and she was elected the Prime Minister. She began talks with the Liberation Tigers of Tamil Eelam (LTTE) with the confidence that she would bring peace to a country torn by war, terrorism and the senseless slaughter of innocents since 1983. But when the Tigers broke the ceasefire in about a year, she had no option but to go to war.

To her disappointment, her six-year 'war for peace' campaign proved fruitless and a war-weary Sri Lanka defeated her party in the 2001 elections, voting instead for Ranil Wickremesinghe. But Kumaratunga herself continued in office as a directly elected Executive President.

In April 2004, Chandrika was catapulted to power again. Mindful of the benefits of a no-war situation, Kumaratunga continued with the peace process with the LTTE.

A long-standing friend of India, Chandrika believes that India should be deemed South Asia's 'engine of growth'.

SOUTH ASIA, OR WHAT IS KNOWN AS SOUTH ASIA TODAY, CONSISTED OF CLOSELY INTER-RELATED KINGDOMS WITH A CIVILISATION DATING BACK TO WELL OVER FOUR millennia. The epicentre of South Asian civilisation in ancient times were the great Mohenjodaro and Harappan civilisations of the Indus Valley. Our ancestors living in these periods invented burnt brick as well as sophisticated irrigation and flood control systems which demonstrate a high level of technological development. The political and social systems were based on highly organised and unified structures, with foreign relations and international trade being conducted from around the third millennia BC.

The Indo-Aryan influx that took place across the Himalayan Massif around 1750 BC brought with it new religions, philosophies and social institutions enriching the great Indian civilisations. The Rig Veda, the two great Indian epics – the Mahabharata and the Ramayana – and the Tamil Sangam texts, as much as available archaeological evidence, amply reveal the sweep and richness of the civilisations and cultures across the subcontinent, from the Himalaya through the Ganges valley, spreading right across the islands of Sri Lanka and the Maldives.

The saga of the subcontinent's cultural odyssey is seen to continue in the Upanishads, the emergence of Jainism and the teachings of the Buddha which have so profoundly shaped the history, culture and the way of life of my own country.

During this entire period of South Asia's history, diverse waves of population influx saw the mixing of varied ethnic, religious and linguistic groups, in a flexible and changing, yet harmonious manner. Ancient socio-political structures in our region evolved to accommodate the ever-changing situations caused by the constant migration of groups of people from across the borders. Independent and socially cohesive – mainly rural and some urban communities – lived and worked as separate and largely self-sufficient units, all of them bound together under the pervasive authority of the king or the prince who was the head of a strongly unified political entity.

The politico-economic structures and organisations of ancient South Asian societies have been studied and written about by philosophers and thinkers such as Karl Marx, Karl August Wittfogel and many other more recent thinkers and researchers. Marx evolved the theory of an 'Asiatic Mode of Production' to distinguish the ancient Asian systems which he believed possessed specific and different economic arrangements from other known economic systems in ancient Europe, Africa or South America.

It is clear that various South Asian societies evolved for many long centuries along similar systems, within a common socio-economic, political and cultural framework. Diverse groups and communities of peoples have lived side by side, in complementary interaction and without conflict, under the unified authority of a sovereign.

It may be interesting to note here that modern historical and archaeological research disproves the theories of an Aryan/Dravidian divide through different historical periods and that the constant influx and outflow of peoples within the subcontinent have blurred categories through the inevitable inter-mixing of human beings.

Diversity was not the inevitable cause of conflict in ancient South Asia. The transformation of diversity into sources of friction seems to have arisen in the colonial era when ethnic, linguistic and religious diversities began to be used and transformed from being the cultural strength of South Asia to its political weakness. The colonial rulers perfected the art of exacerbating and transforming diversity into conflict for their benefit. The Upanishads, the Laws of Manu, the principles of Jainism, Sikhism, Islam and the teachings of the Buddha, on which were based the edicts of emperor Ashoka of the Mauryan Dynasty, all celebrated diversity as being a part of the cosmic order and its equilibrium. All these philosophies recognised and accepted the existence of separate social groups with different caste and social structures. Yet, they were all believed to be knitted together by a common humanity in search of the ultimate reality.

With the advent of colonialism, however, diversity was no more celebrated and accepted as part of an existential necessity but was seen as something to be opposed. Of course, it was greatly advantageous to the invading rulers to divide us in order to rule and dominate us better.

But have we in South Asia realized the vast and massive potential that lies within our boundaries, in our seas, our rivers, our lands and in our human resources that we have lost due to the continuation of division and conflict amongst us?

What have we done about this since the seven modern South Asian states gained independence over half a century ago? Bharat of former times has today become three separate states of India, Pakistan and Bangladesh. Most of our South Asian nation-states are riven by internal conflicts – be they of ethnic or religious origin. The upsurge of ethnic and religious conflict has become the single most dominant political phenomenon of post-independent and post Cold War South Asia.

I strongly believe that our own brand of civilisation and historical development gives us, South Asians, ample models to build unity in diversity. In this context I would have preferred it if the title of talk was 'Unity in Diversity' rather than Unity and Diversity. In no way should the multifarious diversities existing within our region and our nation-states be a cause for division. The very richness of that diversity is our strength and could prove to be so in the future if it is properly guided towards development and prosperity.

The second part of the subject assigned to me happens to be 'Keeping South Asia Together'.

To keep something together, it is presupposed that the relevant thing is already together. As it stands today, can we say that South Asia is together?

Permit me to make bold to state that there are only a few major factors that keep South Asia apart, such as the differences that have occurred between some of the states in our South Asian community.

I daresay that we have undertaken many efforts to bring our nations closer together but we have to do much more.

I propose that we envisage the building of a strong regional union of South Asia. In order to achieve the dream of the vast majority of our peoples for a strong system of regional cooperation, I believe that the one single most essential factor is the political will of our respective governments. I despair at times at the lack of forward movement in this field. I seriously wonder sometimes whether we all realise the massive potential that is contained in a union of South Asian states. Are we at all convinced about this? Can we hope that we could all commit ourselves to this great and noble vision?

I daresay that we have done much towards this, beginning with the *Constitution of India*, which embeds the timeless principles of human rights and secularism. The philosophy of Mahatma Gandhi, as translated by Dr B. R. Ambedkar, into an inclusive and pragmatic institution which is today the *Constitution of India* has proved to be the source of inspiration to the entire region in encouraging us to adopt the humanist values of our collective legacy and to steer away from chauvinism, sectarianism and fundamentalism of various types. We have given birth to our own regional organisation, the South Asian Association for Regional Cooperation, better known as SAARC, and kept it alive under trying and challenging circumstances. Yet, this is not enough. Most of us would like to see SAARC alive, dynamic and proactive. To this end, South Asia must soon resolve the existing conflicts within our states and between them.

India and Pakistan have made serious efforts at resolving the cause of the conflict between their nations. The recent efforts undertaken towards this end are most encouraging to us all in South Asia. We know that the resolution of this long-standing problem requires much goodwill and innovation on both sides and, more than all else, vision and courage from its leaders. I have no doubt that the governments and the leaders of both states possess these qualities in abundance.

In the process of strengthening SAARC we can draw on the numerous successful experiences in other regions of the world. The

European Union affords us many useful examples. I find it fascinating to note that ancient Europe, riven by multifarious divisions and conflicts which gave rise to so many wars between European nations right through the modern history of Europe stretching back about ten centuries, has succeeded at the seemingly impossible task of welding together a large number of European states, formerly in constant conflict with each other, into the highly successful and dynamic European Union with a common Parliament, common tax structure, common passport, a single currency and so many other essential features of a common and single legal, political and administrative unit.

Is it then not possible for us South Asians, with much more commonalities right from our origins, to forge a new unity despite our diversities?

SAARC has the potential of unifying South Asia and converting it into an economic powerhouse in the global world economy. It is the scaffolding on which we could build our unity. It is sorely under-exploited. We all know that nearly one fourth of the world's population lives in South Asia. It is the world's single largest market with a staggeringly vast and empowered middle class.

We take pride in the great achievements of our ancestors in evolving sophisticated language systems, highly developed bodies of literature, sophisticated art forms as demonstrated by our paintings, sculptures and architecture, as well as some of the world's most advanced technologies in architecture, irrigation, flood control, agriculture, manufacturing industries and so on. We also often repeat that all this technology and development was destroyed during centuries of colonial rule.

Yet, South Asian nations have enjoyed political independence for over half a century and we have not yet been able to reach many of the goals successfully achieved by other nations which did not, at the outset, possess the advantages we initially started off with.

The most successful approach perhaps would be to proceed in parallel along several tracks. Major irritants could be handled at the highest political levels while economic and social cooperation is developed at an accelerated pace at other levels. I see no option other than the acceptance by all member states of the policy of close cooperation in economic and cultural spheres as well as in people-to-people contact, even though there may exist political differences between member states.

We have to search for practical tools that could help us along the path. Could we not commence with the United Nations Millennium Development Goals Programme? A joint effort to strengthen individual programmes of each member state could prove to be an excellent starting point for the promotion of close cooperation between us.

We know that poverty alleviation is at the core of most of our development programmes. The Millennium Development Goals Programme has been designed to effectively alleviate poverty. In South Asia, fundamental areas concerning human development, which is dealt with extensively in the Millennium Programme, show even today a weak level of performance. Permit me to quote from the recent *Human Development Report 2004* of UNDP just issued:

- The rate of life expectancy is the lowest and infant mortality the highest in South Asia than in the entire developing world.
- The annual population growth rate of South Asia is also the highest in the world.
- The numbers of those with access to improved sanitation is lower in South Asia than in the rest of the world.
- Adult literacy is the lowest in the world.
- GDP is also the lowest in South Asia as compared with the developing world.
- The number of telephone lines is less than half.
- The number of internet users seven times less in South Asia than in the developing countries as a whole.

These are symptoms that indicate a very serious fault in our systems. They affect the richest resource of South Asia – our people.

Therefore, it is evident that investment in human resource development is the most urgent need of the hour. India's investment in some areas of scientific development, for instance, in information technology illustrates the heights we can reach, given the right policies, conditions and opportunities.

Sri Lanka has also achieved notable success in the areas of human development. Our rates of life expectancy, infant mortality, population growth and adult literacy have reached levels comparable with the developed world, even while our economy still remains weak with moderate GDP growth and per capita income. The reasons adduced to this anomalous situation is that Sri Lankan governments adopted policies with a clear focus on human development.

I would like to propose that an effective platform for building close regional cooperation could be the UN Millennium Development Goals Programme, which was unanimously accepted by all member states of the UN.

The seven member states of SAARC have commenced the process of drawing up action plans under the UN Millennium Development Goals Programme.

All these concern areas of human development. It is conceivable that SAARC formulates regional programmes and plans of action complementary to the national plans, having identified areas for urgent, practical cooperation and mutual assistance between members in order to strengthen and enhance their national programmes. This would involve a vast array of actions in the spheres of education, health, economic infrastructure, strengthening rural entrepreneurs, cultures and overall policy making and good governance.

If we are to achieve these objectives, the institutions of SAARC must be strengthened, beginning with the Secretariat. The latter needs to be expanded and financially strengthened and given more authority in the economic development areas. Fears that some may entertain with regard to political interference in the affairs of member states can be met if a strengthened Secretariat is given powers for action mainly in areas concerned with economic development.

History gives us innumerable examples of instances where conflicts between nations and states have found resolution gradually through social, economic and trading interactions. The people-to-people contact and the networks of common interests created thereby generate a bedrock of mutual interest and trust on which begins to be founded, at a later stage, more sophisticated and organised working arrangements such as regional associations and unions.

Hence, what I propose is not new. It is not greatly innovative. I simply venture to suggest that we let history move along its natural course by removing the unnecessary obstacles that we, humans, have placed in its path. The obstacles of sectarianism or narrow political interests pales into insignificance when placed on the larger canvas of national interest and the great vision of South Asian regional unity. Then there would be no limits to what a united South Asia could achieve together. I have worked closely for over ten years with all South Asian leaders. I am fully aware that every one of them strongly espouses the cause of South Asian unity.

Last year the former Prime Minister of India Mr Atal Behari Vajpayee made a historic statement that, 'Once we reach that stage we would not be far from mutual security, cooperation, open borders and even a single currency.' Prime Minister Manmohan Singh made it clear in his speech here that the present government possesses a similar vision. The leaders of the other SAARC nations have expressed similar views at various times during the past years.

SAARC arrived at an essential point in its regional cooperation when it signed the framework treaty on SAFTA[1] in January this year at Islamabad. We have set ourselves the target of finalising the details so that the Treaty will become operational by 2006. I must also caution here that SAFTA may not automatically lead to enhancement of intra-regional trade. We need to adopt further measures for trade facilitation in order to ensure that our countries achieve the full benefits of SAFTA.

The present conjuncture in the globalised economy is proving to us that global, multilateral trade processes such as the WTO[2] could

1 South Asian Free Trade Agreement.

2 World Trade Organisation.

be extremely disadvantageous to the developing countries. This affords a new relevance to regional cooperation. The success of regional organisations such as ASEAN[3], the European Union and others, strengthen us in our resolve to achieve a closer regional alliance. An effectively operational SAFTA would serve as a take-off point for a wider South Asian economic cooperation.

It may be relevant here to mention that intra-SAARC trade remains at a shockingly low 5 per cent compared, for instance, with 38 per cent within the ASEAN region.

I shall now summarise my proposals for an action plan for South Asian unity.

Firstly, to do all that is required to keep to the targets: to make SAFTA operational by 2006 together with the adoption of other measures required for trade and economic cooperation.

Secondly, formulate effective regional action plans within the UN Millennium Development Goals Programme and implement them within a limited timeframe. Thereby we would successfully alleviate much of the poverty which is the scourge of our region.

Thirdly, formulate action plans for achieving the targets set out in the SAARC Social Charter relating to poverty alleviation, health, education, women, youth and children. We must note here that the Millennium Development Goals Programme covers most of these areas. We could, therefore, include the targets set out in the SAARC Social Charter with the National and Regional Action Plans for the Millennium Development Goals Programme.

Next, we still have a long way to go in successfully achieving the targets set out in the SAARC Convention for Child Welfare and Trafficking in Women and Children for Prostitution. We must address this urgently.

Our region must accelerate existing programmes to liberate and uplift women. Development programmes which do not solicit the active participation of our women and youth in our countries will not reach their potential in poverty alleviation and overall development of our society.

3 Association of Southeast Asian Nations.

We must also adopt more innovative programmes for people-to-people contact in our region. No doubt the business community, the lawyers and the judiciary and the accountants in our region within the SAARC organisation cooperate effectively within their regional associations.

We must also now promote cooperation between other groups of professionals, intellectuals, artists and, why not, the politicians at various levels. I think that interaction between politicians within our region still remains at a most unsatisfactory level. I would say there is an urgent need to promote interaction amongst this group because, after all, it is they who decide finally all policies – national, regional and international. Mutual understanding and awareness of each other's problems will certainly help to reduce tensions in the region.

We must also begin to look at possible arrangements for strengthening regional security cooperation. This probably would prove to be most difficult under the present circumstances of prevailing tensions in our region. But it is also, therefore, a necessity. Varying systems of cooperation in security matters could be designed and adopted between different states with the objective of finally reaching regional security cooperation at a later stage.

In conclusion, it may be pertinent to state once more that cultural heritage need not be a divisive force. We must, and I believe we can, ensure that our diverse cultures, yet our common heritage contain the seeds of unity within that diversity. If we work together we can draw strength from the richness of our civilisational traditions in order to give life to a new and modern South Asian unity. I truly believe that today we have arrived at the threshold of effective action to realise the dreams and aspirations of our people; freedom from poverty, ignorance, under-development and from constant conflict which could best be achieved through regional unity of South Asian states.

Moderator | **Vikram Chandra**

Senior Editor, NDTV

Q&A

Vikram Chandra: Not long before you took charge ten years ago, the relations between India and Sri Lanka were fairly strained. Now they are described as excellent in most ways – diplomatically, economically, strategically. How did the transformation take place, because that might contain some lessons for other strained bilateral relations in this region?

Chandrika Kumaratunga: Well I think it is simple. It was a clear policy that the Sri Lankan governments in the last ten years adopted for closer cooperation and friendly relations with India, backed by similar policies by Indian governments and, of course, a lot of goodwill right down from the leaders to everybody else.

Venkatnarayan ***(Senior Journalist):*** **Could you tell us something about the efforts you are making to restart the peace process, which seems to be taking a long time?**

Chandrika Kumaratunga: It is a long story but to be very brief, in the past ten years successive Sri Lankan governments have espoused the policy of resolving the conflict, the ethnic conflict, through negotiations and a negotiated political settlement rather than through military conflict.

We have done much to persuade the LTTE to stop fighting and to come for negotiations. In the last ten years we have had three, four efforts at negotiations with the LTTE. The negotiation starts, it breaks down, it starts again, and fighting begins. There have been four serious efforts in the last ten years alone and several others before that.

At the moment there is a cease-fire agreement which has held for nearly three years – the longest ever since the military conflict began twenty years ago and it is holding more or less all right. But there are some violations by the LTTE such as child conscription, which does not happen hugely, and to a certain extent, killing of democratic, political Tamil leaders and activists goes on from time to time. Apart from that it is holding.

We have brought in the government of Norway as facilitators. There is a group of monitors, international monitors, led by Norway that is monitoring the cease-fire agreement process in the north and east of the country. There are shortcomings but it is moving forward. I will not say it is a negative movement taking the whole process backwards. The LTTE keeps stating that they are committed to a negotiated settlement and that they will not go back to war and so forth.

For the first time they have stated that they are willing to explore – not accept, but explore – federal solutions in place of the separate state that they have been demanding for twenty long years. So, there is movement forward but they broke off the negotiations with the government one and a half years ago and are still refusing to come to the table even though my government, which came back to power seven months ago has been extremely flexible. They are still rather dogmatic about certain matters and have refused to come to the negotiating table. Still, we keep trying and we have not lost hope completely. Recent developments have given us a little bit more hope than in the last few months that they may be persuaded to begin talks but I cannot say more than that.

Kanwar Khalid Younis *(Member of Parliament, MQM, Pakistan):* Karachi is the financial capital of Pakistan and expects a lot out of SAFTA. Unfortunately from what we have heard from the Finance Minister of India, he is not very hopeful as far as SAFTA is concerned. What is your opinion about the future of SAFTA?

Chandrika Kumaratunga: I am sorry I wouldn't like to comment on a speech I have not heard and unfortunately I could not be present when Mr Chidambaram made his speech. I do not know what he exactly he said.

Vikram Chandra: What is your opinion about the future of SAFTA?

Chandrika Kumaratunga: It is with a lot of difficulty that we were able to finally sign the framework treaty on SAFTA. That in itself is a great achievement and we have given ourselves the target of completing the SAFTA agreement in another one and half years. I think these are good targets. The seven nations, though some of our nations had some doubts about SAFTA because of certain tensions between some countries, have now resolved to move forward and I noticed this at Islamabad in January this year.

It is possible to move forward but the SAARC Secretariat and others have to move it. This year the SAARC Chair has gone to Nepal and ever since they took charge, there have been so many internal problems there. I don't know how much time the leadership of Nepal has had to devote to SAFTA and SAARC matters. But we have seen a lot of commitment to taking SAFTA forward from all the nations.

India's potential for manufacturing and engineering is simply colossal and it is no surprise that foreign direct investments are rising: the world sees India as a growing opportunity.

The Changing
World

■
John Major
■

John Major

Former Prime Minister, United Kingdom

The youngest British Prime Minister of the twentieth century (from 1990-97), John Major succeeded Margaret Thatcher as leader of the Conservative party.

Born on 29 March 1943, Major attended the Rutlish Grammar School, a state-run school for bright children but left at the age of sixteen to apply – unsuccessfully – for a job as a bus conductor. He got his first job as a clerk in an insurance broking firm in 1959 and eventually went on to work at the Standard Chartered Bank where he rose quickly through the ranks, leaving only after his election to Parliament.

Major made two unsuccessful attempts to win a Parliamentary seat before he succeeded, in 1979, when he was elected as a member of the Conservative party from Huntingdonshire.

The early eighties saw an upswing for Major, in 1983 he was made Assistant Government Whip and in 1984, a full-fledged Whip. It was during this time that he was noticed by Margaret Thatcher.

Following Nigel Lawson's resignation as Chancellor of the Exchequer over differences with Thatcher on the impending economic union of the European Community, Major was chosen to replace him, presenting his first budget in 1990.

When Michael Heseltine's challenge to Thatcher's leadership forced her to resign as Prime Minister a few months later in November 1990, Major emerged as a strong candidate to succeed her. After a brief campaign, in which he was opposed by Heseltine and the then Foreign Secretary Douglas Hard but backed by Thatcher herself, Major was appointed Prime Minister on 28 November 1990.

He had his work cut out for him: the world economy was sliding into recession, the Conservative party was racked with infighting and a bitterly anti-Europe wing of his own party was opposing integration with Europe.

Major led his party to victory in the 1992 elections. In 1997, however, the party was defeated by the Labour party and Major had to resign. He finally stood down in the elections of 2001.

I WATCH FROM AFAR INDIA'S GROWING IMPORTANCE WITH ADMIRATION AND PLEASURE – EXCEPT PERHAPS THE ALL TOO FREQUENT OCCASIONS WHEN YOU BEAT MY COUNTRY in cricket, a feeling my friends in Australia will understand only too well.

In the seventeenth century, the English poet John Donne wrote, 'No man is an island, entire of itself.'

Today, over three hundred years later, that is more true than ever. Politics and trade have a global reach. Telecommunications takes the most remote corners of the world right into our own homes. There is no hiding place – and nor will there ever be again. We live in a world without economic boundaries. Once crumbling they are now gone. Politically, we are living through a revolution that is reshaping the distribution of power in ways scarcely imaginable even a decade ago.

When the Soviet Union collapsed and superpower rivalry ended, we all believed the world was safer. It was. The threat of a nuclear exchange between superpowers had clearly fallen away. What we did not realise was that this global security came at a price. It unleashed far greater regional instability and foreshadowed a shifting map of the world.

Let me put some flesh upon that assertion. If the Soviet Union had not collapsed would we have had the bitter civil wars of Bosnia and Kosovo? No, we would not. If the Soviet Union had not collapsed, would the European Union have just enlarged by ten more members states, many of them formerly Iron Curtain countries under Russian domination? Absolutely not. And if the Soviet Union had not collapsed, would we now be engaged in what we euphemistically call the war on terror, knowing that to win it we would have to force out terrorist cells from their safe havens in countries that were once in the Soviet sphere of influence? Again, I doubt it very much.

Ultimately, political authority is the child of economic success. And the economic success of our age is the continuing rise of Asia. In years to come, the majority of world growth, for the first time since 1820, looks set to come from the East and not the West. This trend began with Japan in the 1960s, was followed by the Asian Tiger economies and, more recently, by China.

No one should be surprised by that. China, rather like India, is a very ancient civilisation. The Chinese were making silk and using a potter's wheel before the Egyptians built the Pyramids and before the ancient Britons built Stonehenge.

China's decline as a world power started in the early nineteenth century when she failed to have an industrial revolution. Now she is having one and is maximising her natural advantages. China has space, raw materials, an apparently inexhaustible supply of competitive, cheap labour and is importing technology skills daily. She is buying oilfields, petrochemical facilities, technology, mineral and natural resources and is buying in Western enterprise whenever she needs it.

It is a wondrous sight: I confess I never thought that I would see it in my life, of a once closed Communist economy marching out into the free enterprise world. And where China is today economically, I expect India to be tomorrow.

In the early centuries, India was way ahead of China. Early Chinese travellers to Ashoka's empire were amazed by the sophisticated system of government, the advanced society, the peaceful culture that they found in India. Then, of course, Buddhism became one of the first great exports of India's civilisation across much of Asia.

The history of India's leadership, of the then known world, the dominance of India's cultural and intellectual values goes back to many thousands of years. And it is from this early period that the world owes to India its knowledge of mathematics, apparent again today as India leads the world in so much information technology software. Even as recently as 1700, India had nearly one quarter of the output of the entire world. Now that is relevant because today once more India is in the midst of an explosion of ambition. There is a foolish mantra that the world goes to China for manufacturing and to India for services.

This myth arises in part because of India's success in cornering a large part of the market in knowledge-based industries: in research and development, in information technology, in biotechnology and in the molecular biology. But India's potential for manufacturing and engineering is simply colossal and it is no surprise that foreign direct investments are rising: the world sees India as a growing opportunity.

In the next thirty to forty years much will change in India and little will stay the same.

I have no doubt that within a few years India will become a permanent member of the UN Security Council. The present permanent five are no longer representative without new additions. They were appointed in a different age in a much smaller United Nations. Today changes are necessary and India is an obvious candidate to join them.

I also foresee India joining the G8 Group of Industrial Nations, if logic has meaning. Indeed it would be absurd if she does not since within thirty years or so, it is likely that India's economy will be larger than that of France or Germany or the United Kingdom or Japan.

This is a big change because in the last quarter of a century, the principal engines of world growth have been the US, Japan and the European Union. Soon, China, non-Japanese Asia and India will join them. As a result, growth in the world economy will be better balanced than it has ever been before and following from that, political power will be more widespread.

The effect of this scenario foreshadows a far larger role for India. If you could add economic muscle to the world's largest democracy you have a potent force. China has burst into prominence. India is poised to do so and within thirty years she will be as influential in the world as she has been at any time in her history.

In our fast changing world, there are two conflicts that have proved to be immensely divisive. Upon Iraq, history offers us some valuable insights. In 1914, Britain invaded and occupied Mesopotamia to protect oil interests in Persia. The British created 'modern' Iraq out of Mesopotamia and the governates of Baghdad, Basra and Mosul. It was nation building and yet Britain was regarded as a 'foreign occupier' and faced widespread rebellion before she was able to establish an indigenous government and then leave. And behind her in a war cemetery in Baghdad she left the heavy price of occupation.

Today in Iraq we have an interim administration planning to hold elections in January to create a democratically elected government to take Iraq into the future. Many questions lie ahead and none of them are easy. The first is whether the conditions will exist in January to allow the elections to an assembly to be held? The date has been fixed.

The determination to hold those elections is evident but so are the problems. There has been no census. There is no register of voters. Nor, crucially, is there law and order on the streets.

If there is chaos in Najaf or Fallujah, is it possible for them to vote? If they cannot vote, and deputies to the assembly have to be 'appointed' rather then elected, would the elections be seen as legitimate in Iraq or outside Iraq? I doubt, for example, if the presidential election in the US would have been considered as valid if Texas and California had been unable to vote.

It is absolutely right to aim for an election in January – but the problems to be overcome are legion and it would be quite an achievement if it can successfully be done on schedule. But let us assume that even if they are held, what then? Who will win more seats in the Assembly and who will have the right to form the government? Probably a combination of many factions of Shi'ites, since they collectively form 70 per cent of the electorate.

This begs a whole range of questions. Will the Kurds accept an outcome? Will the Sunnis? They have both feared and distrusted the Shi'ites for generations. It will take skilful political handling to form a government that is welcomed by the populace in Iraq, rather than one that might lead to civil unrest or – at worst – even civil war? The new Iraqi government's first job will be to draft a new Constitution.

The dilemma here is crystal clear: if power is held centrally, will any government obtain the consent of the regions to govern?

Alternatively, if the Constitution is a federal one – with power devolved to the regions and with Shi'ite, Sunni or Kurd governors running their own regions – is there then the risk of secession and the break-up of Iraq?

And, in particular, would the long-term Kurdish ambition for a Kurdistan be irresistible? And – if so – how would Turkey react to that development? The answers to these worrying questions are unclear. And then, of course, is the question: what is the future of the coalition? Can they leave Iraq? If they do leave, what do they do if chaos breaks out? If they stay, will this radicalise Islam even more than at present?

I set out these questions to emphasise the complexities involved in the present situation. The intention to create a democratic Iraq is the right one, a noble objective. If successful, a democratic Iraq next door to a democratic Turkey would be a powerful impetus to the entire region. But we are still very far from that outcome.

The second Middle East conflict is upon the issue that is, above all, the poison in the well of relations with Islam: Palestine.

Today, with uncertainties of policy and personality, is not the occasion for widespread analysis except to note that Israel and the Palestine need a settlement. An active peace process is vital – without one there is a vacuum and into that, terror and mayhem step too readily.

We have seen too much of that in recent years as a low grade war has simmered always at the risk of becoming a full-scale war. Wicked men have encouraged foolish young men and women to become human bombs in Israel and provoke retaliation and then counter retaliation. Hope has fled.

The destruction of hope is all too often the product of intolerance and terrorism is the sharpest expression of fear and mistrust that intolerance thrives on.

On 9 September 2001, terrorism over-reached itself and America and democracy retaliated.

This war on terror is unlike any conflict we have seen in modern times. It is more complex and may be more protracted than any conventional war. But it affects us all and should involve us all: it is not just a war for the US but for every democracy. For, in the mind of terrorist, no one – and no place – is immune. Not New York, nor Baghdad, not Madrid and not even New Delhi.

Can such a concept of war be won? With one caveat, yes it can. The caveat is that terrorist groups are rarely entirely destroyed: they spilt and smaller groups, sometimes made up of the hardest of hard-liners, tend to replace them. But it is possible to diminish terrorism and destroy its potency and its threat.

But here then is another dilemma in achieving that outcome. To win this war a collaborative effort is vital. The cooperation is needed of all governments to deny terrorist groups the safe havens in which they so often hide and find comfort. All those who can, must work together to address the grievances that enable extremist groups to paint the developed world in unflattering terms, and which act as recruiting sergeants for terrorism.

Let me now turn to an issue that must be for all of us a moral and an economic imperative. Poverty is not an evil in itself: it fuels despair and can be a recruiting sergeant for terrorism. At minimum, it offers a ready ear for those who wish to spread hatred against richer and more developed nations.

As we look forward, we should assess the political, social and economic long-term problems which will beset us if rich developed nations continue to get richer and undeveloped nation fall yet further behind.

In some parts of the world, corruption and poverty condemn untold millions to a life of misery and hardship. Some people may rather dismissively say, 'Well, that is *their* problem. Bad government, bad economic decisions, bad judgments made this problem.' Well, maybe, but that is not true in every case. And *their* problem? Hardly.

One *half* of the world's population is under twenty-four: in no way can they be held responsible for the conditions in which they live. And in any event, the world as a whole is having to live with the resentment, bitterness and political hostility that poverty causes amongst those outside the circle of prosperity.

Our world has a population of six billion people. Of these six billion, one half – three billion people – live on less than $2 a day and one fifth live on less than $1 a day. The disparity of *their* life with that of someone on even the lowest levels of social support in the developed nations is stark.

The rich nations do much to help but not, I think, as much as is needed. Far more is needed. Collectively the rich nations spend $50 billion a year on overseas aid – a truly enormous sum of money but less generous than it seems when you realise that Europe and America alone spend $350 billion just on agricultural subsidies. That is, to put it more bluntly, seven times as much for subsidising food for those who are well fed than the whole world spends on all the needs of those whose bellies are so often empty.

It is a statistic that is even more bizarre when you realise such subsidies often cut away the possibility of the poorest nations in the world selling their agricultural products into the developed markets. It seems to me that if it is right to wage war on terror – and it *is* right to wage war on terror – then it is equally right to wage war on poverty and on hardship.

Moreover, if nothing is done the problem will worsen. In the next twenty-five years, world population is likely to grow from the present six billion people to eight billion people. Of the extra two billion, 97 per cent will be in that part of the world that has an income below $2 a day.

This, frankly, is not sustainable if we wish our children to inherit a world free of conflict. Nor is it moral.

In the 1940s or 1950s – after a very different sort of war to those we contemplate today – America launched a plan to deliver aid and rescue Europe from the devastation of the Second World War. It was, as Winston Churchill said, 'The most unsordid act in history.' Not even the great wealth of America could do that alone these days. But in the world in which there is wealth at a level undreamt of by earlier generations – the developed nations collectively must soon consider another such 'unsordid act'.

It will come because it cannot be ignored. The question is when will it come? If the rich nations act early, act out of conscience not only can they foreclose on misery and hardship to come, but they can undercut the breeding ground of terror that at present is such a threat to international security and prosperity.

Today, we have a global economy. The political map is more fluid than it has ever been in my life. Daily, there are exciting new developments in technology and communications. The speed of medical advancement is as bewildering as the demand for medical services is infinite. Yet it will grow: the mapping of the human genome system will lead to an explosion of demand for preventive care and, where this is provided, to a sharp increase in life expectancy.

There is a pattern in all aspects of our life. Science and technology is accelerating change which already takes place at break-neck speed. What might this mean for our new century? What scale of change can we envisage? Without a crystal ball, one can look back to the past for clues.

At the beginning of the twentieth century, no one knew of blood groups, of hormones, or barbiturates. Vacuum cleaners and household detergents still lay in the future. Marie Curie had not discovered radium nor had Albert Einstein perfected his theory of relativity. Count Zeppelin[1] was designing a machine that would fly, but it would be another twenty-seven years before Colonel Lindbergh[2] would fly from America to France. At the beginning of the twentieth century, few people, if anyone, would have ever dreamt that there would come a day when you could breakfast in London and dine in Delhi.

In 1900, politically, the Europeans were dominant. The UK, France and Russia controlled 80 per cent of the world surface. The US was a debtor nation financed largely by the city of London. How things have changed.

The age of empire is over. The Ottoman Empire has gone. The Austro-Hungarian Empire has gone. The French Empire has gone.

---

1 Ferdinand Adolf August Heinrich von Zeppelin.

2 Charles Lindhberg who flew non-stop from New York to Paris on the Spirit of St Louis on 20-21 May 1927.

The British Empire has gone. The Russian Empire has both come and gone.

The US is now the most powerful nation in the world with the two most populous nations, China and India – both on course to becoming great economic powers within the next three decades.

Europe is wholly different, building unity on the back of one thousand years of war and has established the richest and largest free trade area in history – from Ireland in the West to the very borders of Russia in the East. The European Union has been too insular for much of its lifetime, but, as it enlarges and moves, it is becoming more outward looking – not at least in its dialogue with Asia.

Russia, herself, now lifts more oil each day than Saudi Arabia and is blessed with one-third of the world's supply of natural gas. Brazil and Turkey and, perhaps, Mexico are emerging as future economic forces. The impact of this is not simply on economics and on politics.

Children born today will live in a very different world from one in which we grew up. They are likely to see the conquest of the stars. They will live longer and they will see more, do more and know more than any earlier generation. Technology will enable them to see deserts bloom. They will see a genetic rebuilding of failing bodies and they will live with technical innovations beyond our wildest imagination.

It will be a world unrecognisable to their forebears. It will be competitive, complex, confusing – sometimes even brutal. Our task in this generation is to look critically at our world and see it as it is, so that we can try and shape how it could be.

Can we lift our eyes beyond dispute and towards concordat? Beyond the short-term to the problems of the next generation? Beyond self-interest and towards common interest?

We certainly have the ability to do so. The question is: have we the wisdom and have we the will?

Moderator | **Salman Haider**
Former Foreign Secretary

Venkatnarayan (Senior Journalist): Mr Major, based on what was clearly a sexed-up report on non-existent weapons of mass destruction in Iraq, you waged what Kofi Annan has called an illegal war. Yet Mr Bush wins an election and Mr Blair is hoping to win again for the third time in February. What will you do, if a new Parliament in Iraq passes a resolution asking the coalition forces to get out of their country? And what are you going to do if they elect Saddam Hussein president again?

John Major: You made an assumption about the next elections in the UK that Mr Blair will win. I have to say that is not my preferred option. I would be extraordinarily surprised if the Iraqis were to elect Saddam Hussein – even on the unlikely assumption that he was free to contest the election – after his lamentable record over many years.

The other element in your question is the underlying presumption that after the war and after the election, the coalition forces would wish to stay there. That is not my judgment. When there is order and stability and an elected government, there is no active choice of which I am aware, that either the US or the UK or any other member of the coalition would want to stay in Iraq rather than to leave Iraq as a democracy to run its own affairs.

I remember one of the great concerns we had in the first Iraq war was the argument that America and Britain were keen to break up Iraq. Indeed, we spent a great deal of time considering how *not* to breakup Iraq and to leave it as a single entity, so that it might have a more prosperous future. I have no reason to believe that does not remain the policy both in the US and in the UK. We are not seeing here a new act of imperialism where we are searching for a new colony. That is not the world in which we live and this is not the policy either of the US government as I understand it and certainly not the policy, nor the will, nor the likelihood of the British Government and the British Parliament.

Q. Please share your views on how force can be legitimised in international relations without violating the sovereignty of a nation?

John Major: Many of the disputes that concern people – whether you talk of the clash of civilisations or use a number of other euphemisms to effectively mean the same thing – it seems to me are based on a misunderstanding of the general position of Christianity and Islam.

Islam is essentially a peaceful religion. If you go back, for example, to the Crusades, the principal atrocities were by the Crusaders not by the Islamic defenders of the time. What is happening now is that that there is, amongst some terrorist groups – Al-Qaeda being an obvious example – a philosophy that is a perversion of what Islam stands for. If you had Osama bin Laden here today and, it would be extremely convenient to have him here, you would find that the people he hates most in the world are not the Americans nor the British but the Saudi Arabians. His first target would be Saudi Arabia because he represents a position of Islam. Sometimes in the West we make the mistake of running two things – terrorism and fundamentalism – together.

Fundamentalism is not Islam but a position of the Islamic religion. Yet the perverted element of Islam stands in stark contrast not only to the Western world but also to the rest of the Islamic world. I don't think we should let this position continue. We should expose it whenever we can because what we are talking about are people who will murder indiscriminately.

I have spent a long time trying to deal with Irish terrorism in the UK and there is a mindset amongst terrorists which is utterly careless of anything except their own motives and aims.

M.E. Nkoana Mashabane (High Commissioner, South Africa): You have not really dwelt upon the role of Africa. What role do you think Africa plays in this new world order?

John Major: You are quite right, I did not mention Africa and if I had more time I would have done so. I have spent a fair amount of time working in Africa as a young man. I saw a lot of Africa in my youth.

I think that if Africa is to grow as one would wish, one or two nations have to be economically successful – either Nigeria or South Africa. If one of those nations can become an economic success, I think they will act as an economic magnet and that involves a range of things, many of them extremely complex.

I think a lot can be done with Africa. I think it has fallen behind. It does desperately need more political stability than it has had. I don't think that the Africans have been well served by African governments – I speak of sub Saharan Africa.

I daresay many people have not focused on the sheer scale of the AIDS problem in sub Saharan Africa but to give you an illustration, one in eight South Africans probably has the AIDS virus and in tiny Uganda a million people have died of AIDS and another million have it. So working on AIDS is vital for the recovery of Africa.

Prem Shankar Jha (Senior Journalist): Mr Major, you implied that the kind of globalised and inter-dependent world that we are becoming can only actually be governed as a kind of a commonwealth multilaterally and by some kind of large major consensus. How then do you view the present unilateralism of the US? Do you see this as an aberration that is going to correct itself and, if so, how? Also how do you view the kind of survey that shows that about 100,000 people have been killed in Iraq since the war began last year? Is that not too steep a price to pay for gains that are still very much over the horizon?

John Major: My instinct is to prefer a consensus to conflict. But I do not believe in consensus without any price. I have spent too long in the European Union to realise that actually reaching consensus can be pretty hard, if not impossible. Consensus is obviously preferable to conflict but there are times when you have to make decisions and look at those decisions. That is what changes the world – and usually changes it for the better.

As far as the Iraqi conflict is concerned, I do not know where this figure of 100,000 came from. It seems very high to me. I think it has come from one body, it certainly has been challenged by the British military establishment. I think the figure is nothing remotely like that.

On the question of whether America is unilateralist, I do not know if you think it is. I can understand why people are making that assumption but I think if you take the range of American policy you would ask, would an American administration that is unilateralist have voted for, I think, $100 billion for the cure of AIDS in Africa? If they were looking inwardly rather than outwardly, why would they be contributing to the success of another trade round? Why would they be investing outwardly if they were unilateralist? One can always find a policy where you could argue a particular case but I do not think in general this is true.

I seem to recall that both the League of Nations and the UN were essentially an impetus from the US. So the long tradition of America is to be multilateralist and I hope and expect that tradition to continue.

General V.P. Malik (Former Chief of Army): You made a very brief reference to the Security Council when you said it needs to have more members. In that context, how do you see the UN and Security Council in future being able to tackle the problems that you have highlighted, because in recent years the role of the UN appears to have got eroded somewhat.

John Major: The point I was making about the Security Council – and I think these figures are from memory, so they might be slightly off but not very much – was that when the permanent five as we now know them were appointed, self-appointed one might say, the membership of the UN was about 49 nations. It is now 193 and there is a compelling case for a significant enlargement of the Security Council. I think it would certainly include India, Germany, Japan, probably Brazil and one would believe either South Africa or Nigeria to represent Africa.

What I say is now universally accepted. It can no longer continue. It is outdated. Time has moved and it requires reform.

Can the UN, in essence, be made more credible than it has been? Well the answer to that is very straightforward. It depends upon its members. The UN is nothing other than what its members provide it with. If its members will it to be more successful, then it can be more successful. Now there are some people who would say that the UN is very bureaucratic. It is very expensive. It is not very effective. But, if we did not have any international clearinghouse for disputes and discussions like the UN, we would have to invent one. So, I think the concept of getting rid of the UN is a very foolish one.

The concept of reforming it to make it more effective is a wise one. There are areas where it can be made a good deal more effective administratively and more effective in its decision-making process. I think that ought to be the objective and I think a part of that objective would be to reform the Security Council. That makes it seem a more credible option for those nations who look at the present permanent five and think that they are no longer as representative of world power as once they were.

Chinmoy Gharekhan (Former Indian Ambassador to the UN): Very often it is said that South Asia is a nuclear flashpoint. Do you really believe that the leaders in India and Pakistan would be foolhardy enough to go to nuclear war with each other or do you believe that this is just a scare that interested nations are spreading and making others believe in for the sake of their national agenda?

John Major: As far as India and Pakistan are concerned, I think the situation at the moment is more hopeful than it has been for a long time. It looks to me as though the emergence of dialogue and the personalities of the prime minister of India and the president of Pakistan offer a greater possibility for a constructive dialogue that will reach a conclusion we have known for very long time. I certainly would not expect the draconian fear of an exchange of nuclear weaponry. That does not mean that I would not wish to see non-proliferation carried out – not just in India and Pakistan, but elsewhere as well.

Competing in the

Global Economy

■

Kiran Mazumdar-Shaw

■

Mukesh D. Ambani

■

Nandan M. Nilekani

■

Subir Raha

■

Moderator

N.K. Singh

Member, Planning Commission

Kiran Mazumdar-Shaw

Chairman and Managing Director, Biocon India

Whenever Kiran Mazumdar-Shaw looks back on her life, she is bound to recall 2004 as a landmark year. No stranger to accolades, she has received several in the course of her twenty-six year career including a Padma Shri in 1989, Ernst & Young's 'Entrepreneur of the Year Award' for life sciences and healthcare and with the listing of Biocon India on the Bombay Stock Exchange, she has also been ranked the wealthiest woman entrepreneur in India. Just a few weeks after the Hindustan Times Leadership Initiative, Kiran was awarded the Padma Bhushan.

Born in Bangalore and educated at the Bishop Cotton Girls School and then Mount Carmel College, Kiran went on to Ballarat College, Melbourne, specialising in malting and brewing technology to become India's first woman brewmaster.

But life in the male-dominated brewing profession was not easy and so with Rs 10,000 in her bank, she turned to biotechnology, founding Biocon in 1978 in collaboration with an Irish firm.

Today, Biocon India has been transformed from a small enzyme maker into a drug firm that is challenging global insulin makers. In addition to making enzymes and drugs to fight diabetes, cancer and cholesterol, Biocon has separate units offering contract research and clinical trial services for global clients. The company has a team of 1200 technical experts and 130 patents to its credit.

Kiran works with her Scottish husband, John Shaw, who quit his job as a financial expert in Madura garments to become Biocon's Vice-chairman.

Mukesh D. Ambani

Chairman and Managing Director, Reliance Industries Ltd

Chairman and Managing Director of Reliance Industries Limited, India's largest private sector company and a Fortune Global 500 company, Mukesh Ambani is the elder son of Dhirubhai Ambani, founder of the Reliance conglomerate.

In *India Today's* 2003 'power list', Mukesh was ranked number one while he was thirty-three in the list of fifty 'Most Respected Business Leaders of the World' in a Pricewaterhouse Cooper's survey.

After joining Reliance in 1981, he initiated its backward integration from textiles into polyester fibres and further into petrochemicals. In this process, he has directed the creation of sixty new, world-class manufacturing facilities that have raised Reliance's manufacturing capacities from less than a million tonnes to twelve million tonnes per year.

Credited with bringing about financial innovation in the Indian capital markets, Mukesh pioneered India's first foray into the overseas capital markets with an international public offering of global depository receipts, convertibles and bonds. He has directed Reliance in its effort to raise, since 1991, around US$ 2 billion from overseas financial markets.

He is credited with the creation of the world's largest grassroots petroleum refinery at Jamnagar, India.

Currently involved in rolling out the largest and most complex information and communications technology initiative in the world in the form of Reliance Infocomm, Mukesh is also steering Reliance's initiatives on a world scale, offshore, deep water, oil and gas exploration and production programme, a pan-India petroleum retail network involving 5,800 outlets and a research-led life sciences initiative covering medical, plant and industrial biotechnology.

Mukesh is a member of the Prime Minister's Advisory Council on Trade and Industry. He lives in Mumbai with his wife Nita and three children.

Nandan M. Nilekani

CEO, President and Managing Director, Infosys Technologies

Nandan M. Nilekani, CEO of one of the most high-profile Indian software companies, is one of seven Infosys founders. Younger of the two sons of Mohan Nilekani, a manager in Minerva Mills, Nandan spent his first twelve years in Bangalore but due to his father's transferable job moved to his uncle's home in Dharwad to complete his studies.

In 1973, Nandan was admitted to the prestigious Indian Institute of Technology, Mumbai. A day after graduating, he walked into the office of N. R. Narayana Murthy, the then head of the software group at the Mumbai-based Patni Computer Systems, to seek a job. Murthy hired Nandan on the spot.

Just three years later, the seven founders of Infosys decided to launch out on their own with Murthy in the lead. That decision redefined the frontiers of the domestic software industry. At that time, India was still a closed economy with foreign exchange restrictions. But the 1980s and early 1990s saw the team work at a frantic pace to build Infosys.

Today, Infosys is a force to reckon with both in India and abroad. The company recruits only the meritorious 1.5 per cent of the total number of people who apply to it.

Neither riches nor success has changed Nandan who describes himself as a person from small town Dharwad. He has donated $5 million to his alma mater and as Chairman of the Bangalore Agenda Task Force, set up by the Karnataka state government, is contributing his mite – ideas and money – to improving the city's infrastructure.

Subir Raha

Chairman and Managing Director, Oil & Natural Gas Corp. Ltd.

Subir Raha knows the oil sector like the back of his hand. He joined the Indian Oil Corporation as a management trainee in 1970 where he was elevated as a board member in 1998. But that is only a glimpse of his achievements. Today Raha is the Chairman and Managing Director of the $28 billion Oil & Natural Gas Corporation (ONGC) – a corporation that is ranked as the most valuable company in India.

At the forefront of buying oil equity abroad in India's quest for energy security, ONGC Videsh has invested $3.5 billion in acquiring a global footprint – from Vietnam to Sudan to Sakhalin to Australia.

Raha, who graduated in electronics and tele-communication engineering from Jadavpur University and completed his Masters in business management from Leeds, has been an integral part of the Indian oil sector as it has evolved. Before joining the Indian Oil Board, he served as the head of the Oil Coordination Committee, Ministry of Petroleum & Natural Gas. During this assignment, he managed oil and gas logistics and worked on deregulating the sector.

Raha is concurrently the Chairman of ONGC Videsh Ltd – the overseas subsidiary with over $3 billion investment abroad and Mangalore Refinery & Petrochemicals Ltd that was taken over by ONGC in 2003.

His commitment to the oil sector also manifests itself outside business as he is the Chairman of the Petrotech Society – a non-profit organisation for the promotion of academic excellence in Indian oil and gas industry. He also heads the Research Council of the Indian Institute of Petroleum under the Council for Scientific and Industrial Research.

In addition to being the President of the National Petroleum Management, he also heads the Indian Global Compact Society – an initiative of the United Nations, the business community, ILO and NGOs.

N K. SINGH: IT HAS BECOME VERY FASHIONABLE TO DESCRIBE THE GLOBAL ECONOMY AS ONE INTERDEPENDENT SEAMLESS SUPPLY CHAIN IN WHICH PRODUCTION SYSTEMS AND patterns are seamlessly intertwined and to see new centres of economy gratuitously or gradually in terms of market and market forces.

Are corporates bothered by this – and what is it that worries them? Is it the supply side in access to shrinking inputs which includes human resources? Or is it the demand side, namely, access to markets and partially open markets? Or is it that outsourcing – coupled with whatever it represents in terms of the management of the supply chain and desegregation of production into efficient units – is creating new business paradigms to which the corporates would need to respond?

Mukesh Ambani: I believe that the twenty-first century is going to be completely different from the twentieth century. We are on the threshold of a phenomenal growth in this part of the world. In the last hundred years, the world output has grown from $1.6 trillion to $30 trillion dollars. In the next fifty years, it will grow from $30 trillion to $60 trillion dollars – and that is like adding four new US economies.

The good news for us, in this part of the world, is that finally growth has shifted from the developed to the developing economies. If you look at the world – and it is not a perfect place – disparity exists on a huge scale. Even today, in the first decade of the twenty-first century, we have 20 per cent of the world's population having access to 80 per cent of the world's output. Only a billion people are doing well in the world economy while five billion are lagging behind. So, I think that the challenge – and the opportunity – is to catch up. Abolition of poverty no longer remains an empty slogan.

How do we face this? I think that the notion of the world as a village has become a reality. Globalisation is here to stay and we are completely integrated.

The second most important thing that is driving this is technology. And what technology has enabled is the unbundling of industries. Today, you can design a car in the US, engineer it in India, manufacture different components in different parts of the world and market it globally. I can take you industry segment by industry segment where unbundling of the value chain creates opportunities.

Finally, capital and talent both are available and tradable globally and I think that is where our opportunity comes from. It comes from taking India from a $500 billion economy to a $5 trillion economy, and towards that our challenges really are to build systemic capacities. We have an opportunity to build new systemic capacities of governance, systems and process and of individual capabilities that can leapfrog India into the centrestage.

N.K. Singh: So Mukesh is not terribly bothered about the problems this kind of global integrated production demands in market patterns but is overwhelmed, to some extent, by the opportunities that it offers and whether we will be able to meet the challenges of the new opportunities. Kiran, would you agree with that interpretation?

Kiran Mazumdar-Shaw: I share the same kind of enthusiasm for addressing opportunities, but in our field of biotechnology, the key drivers are cost and speed of innovation and pivotal to all that is discovery research.

What we really have to address in India is this shortage of discovery research. I think 1 January is going to be a very important day for us because that is the day we are supposed to be TRIPS compliant[1] and that is when our discovery research attention and focus has to be very strong. India has very good people skills but we have to shift the mindset into that kind of discovery research.

We need to address, as a country, how we are going to build capacity in generating a fountainhead of new ideas or regional research from our research institutes? Industry has to take that forward and commercialise the fountainhead of new ideas. We need to expand our centres of excellence in a dramatic way. We need many, more centres of excellence. We cannot rely on the few that exist today. We need to do that kind of capacity building in terms of human resource.

I am also concerned about our biodiversity policy. We look at biodiversity, as we should, as a good research opportunity. But we

1 Trade-related intellectual property rights.

have a biodiversity policy that is very xenophobic. We are approaching it with a lot of paranoia and with a very protectionist attitude. Whereas today, the entire biotech segment globally is about networking, and I see partnering as a huge opportunity for Indian biotech to be a part of that global opportunity. That is what I am excited about because I think India offers low-cost opportunity for innovation and this is what the West is looking for. India provides a very attractive opportunity to build a strong global biotech segment.

N.K. Singh: Nandan, may I request you to respond to some of the issues which I had raised and to which Mukesh had briefly responded?

Nandan Nilekani: If you look at global development over the last hundred years, you've had a migration of the economies of the

The rise in aspiration is remarkable. We are no longer future.

world from agriculture to industry to services and, increasingly, most modern economies have a high percentage of GDP coming from services.

Now, a combination of things have happened to essentially destabilise the equilibrium that existed. One is what Mukesh referred to as the advancement in global technology, in computers and in communication which has made the entire world a wired, borderless place. Second is the supply chain in which I can move products and people and logistics. For instance, there's movement of capital through global capital markets and the movement of labour through migration. We have a form of fungible world.[2]

Coupled with this has been the addition of India and China to the global economic situation by becoming more market-oriented economies that want to leverage human capital. When you have a

---

2 Fungible: 'Designating movable goods, such as grain or money, any unit or part of which can replace another, as in discharging a debt; interchangeable.' From *The Quintessential Dictionary*.

significant part of world GDP in services and a significant component of those services being what you call as fungible services or services you can deliver over a wire – it does not matter whether you are sitting in Bangalore, Delhi, or the Bahamas – you can actually do high quality value addition to things across the world.

This is a shift in the way things are going to change. The way value is created in the next few years will be fundamentally different from the way it was done for the last few years. Whether it is outsourcing or Business Process Outsources (BPO), the way the world works is changing and we are at the early stages of that revolution. It is a really new business innovation which will impact economies, society, power equations among nations and global security.

resigned to our fate. People are looking for a bright

– Subir Raha

I agree with Mukesh that this is an opportunity that we must not lose. From a strategic perspective, India is uniquely well-positioned to leverage and maximise this changing world because it is the first time that any nation is trying to become a First World Nation by leveraging its human capital. That is a very important point because if you are a nation that has built its economic strength on commodities, it is not really something that is accessible to the population. That is why you see many countries in West Asia, Africa and South America that are very rich in oil but where the people are still living in poor conditions.

But when you have a revolution that is driven by human capital, the only way you are going to win is by taking that human capital to the next level. It is by nature progressive: you have to create a political system and institutions that give good governance, are equitable, provide opportunities to people. The business and global opportunity are driving India towards the kind of India you want to create.

We have everything in our favour. We have the demographics. We have the largest pool of young people anywhere in the world.

N.K. Singh: Subir, would you like to respond to Nandan.

Subir Raha: Well my fellow panelists talked about the great opportunities we have before us in India and perhaps in the region.

A year back, in October last year, Goldman Sachs had released their report on BRICs[3] (Brazil, Russia, India and China) and all of us went gaga because it essentially said that only two of the six economies today who have more than $1 trillion GDP – the US and Japan – will remain in the G-6 by 2050. China, India, Brazil and Russia will replace UK, France, Italy and Germany. There were lots of write-ups and everyone was very thrilled.

But when you go through the entire report, which is available in the public domain,[4] I found something very disturbing which I thought I would share. To validate the model, which was developed to project the macro-economics for the next fifty years, the actual data of forty years, from 1960, was used as inputs. That was run

The way the world works is changing and this is going to nations and global security.

for ten countries, including India, and this model, based on the actual statistics of forty years, brought out that from 1960-2000, India should, or could, have had a rate of GDP growth of around 7.5 per cent. The actual figure was 4.5 per cent or thereabouts. Of all the ten countries, ours had the largest gap between what could have been done and what actually happened.

We have the harsh reality of a lost opportunity for the last forty years. Today, when you talk of the great opportunities for the next fifty years, what has exactly changed? What has changed in politics, economics, systems, society that should give us the confidence that a lost opportunity of forty years will be realised in the next fifty years? We have all these resources: human resource development, an education system, a stable political system

3 Goldman Sachs, *Global Economics Paper No. 99: Dreaming with BRICs: The Path to 2050*. (October 2003).

4 See, for instance, www.gs.com/insight/research/reports.

and a sound industrial base, but we had these in the 60s, 70s, 80s and 90s.

We might have made incremental improvements in these areas but we need to really look at a situation where the world does offer huge opportunities but these are not exclusive to India and are available to anyone who is willing to put in the work and effort. So, we must ensure that we do not repeat the story of the last four decades in the coming decades.

N.K. Singh: What should India do to position itself to take maximum advantage from these new opportunities? Is it low cost infrastructure? Is it cost of efficient financial intermediation? Is it human resource development talent? Or is it a fiscal regime? Mukesh, may I request you to comment on what you believe should be the key ingredients to position India in terms of policy framework that will enable us to derive the maximum advantage from the kind of opportunities which you and Nandan mentioned in your introductory comments?

impact economies, society, power equations among

– Nandan M. Nilekani

Mukesh Ambani: I am very tempted to respond to Subir and say that what has changed is our attitude. That is the most important change I have seen in the past twenty-five years of being in business. There has been a fundamental shift in attitude and mindset which is being driven by younger people. It's an attitude that says, 'Given a chance we will do it.'

Along with this, there is the realisation across all aspects of society, from government to bureaucracy to ordinary people, that government should – and will – stay out of business.

These are two major changes.

What Nandan's industry has achieved gives us an intellectual brand on a worldwide basis: that we in India can deliver, on a yearly basis, superior quality of services. The world recognises that Indians, in terms of talent and professional capability, are second to none.

In thinking about the future and about what government should do, I want to supplement Nandan in what he said: look at our talent.

The Indian population of 1.2 or 1.3 billion in the next twenty years is fast converting from a liability to an asset. In the next twenty years, India will become younger while the world becomes older. The world is forecasting a professional talent shortage in the US, Europe, Japan, Singapore and Australia of more than 35 to 40 million professionals.

India will have 400 million people under the age of 35 with a literacy level of 75 per cent. Clearly, education has to be our priority and education must move beyond elementary education to building skills at an unprecedented level and to ensuring that this is our raw material.

We should really think about our professional talent, or the human talent that we can convert into professional talent, as our equivalent of oil. If we can get 10 million or 15 million of our

We in India can deliver, on a yearly basis, superior quality of talent and professional capability are second to none.

professionals – which is only 2 per cent of our work force – employed for the rest of the world to meet the demand shortage in the next fifteen to twenty years, we would have achieved a transfer of capital of $4 trillion. That is twice as much as what China has achieved in terms of getting capital.

If we single-mindedly focus on harnessing our talent, ensuring that we create a competitive environment that every individual is better than his counterpart in the world, and if we then move from the individual to the corporate level; to the state and government level to building next generation systemic capacities, I think that's a single-minded focus: to treat our human talent in the next twenty years as equivalent to our oil; get the capital and use that capital to build infrastructure. That is what will move the bottom of the pyramid of our population to a higher quality of life and that is how we can change India.

N.K. Singh: There is some commonality and some asymmetry. The commonality is that Mukesh is beginning to focus on one key component: how to convert India's young population from not being a

demographic drag by investing in human resource development and by inculcating skills necessary to meet India's needs and global needs. Kiran, you seemed more sceptical in your remarks that there has to be a major change in the mindset. Were you speaking from a specific dimension or were you talking about a change in the mindset that has to be brought about in the more generic sense?

Kiran Mazumdar-Shaw: At a broad level I agree that there has been a terrific attitudinal change and a new sense of confidence. India certainly has a can-do attitude but I am speaking more from a sector specific kind of observation where I really believe that we need to see a mindset change in our research laboratories. That is the fountainhead of new ideas and that is where we would like to see a huge attitudinal change in order to partake in the global community and global business.

of services. The world recognises that Indians, in terms

– Mukesh D. Ambani

We have to be very aggressive about good innovation and at the moment, I do not see much of that happening. We are also trying to see how industry and academia starts partnering more aggressively and I am confident that the moment we comply with TRIPS on 1st January, we are going to see a huge shift in the mindset because I always believe that India delivers strongly when you are forced into a position. I expect a lot of change to take place from next year onwards.

I am not sceptical but we need to do a lot because at the broad level we are very enthusiastic, our aspirations have changed and there is a huge positive mindset change but I would like to see more of this change taking place at the very basic level.

N.K. Singh: So, some attitudinal changes have taken place but more needs to be done particularly in the area of intellectual property rights. Nandan, what would be your priorities to which we need to attach importance to derive the maximum advantage from the opportunities of globalisation and, as Mukesh pointed out, to the human resource development area?

Nandan Nilekani: Investing in human capital and the fact that we have so many young people is critical to what we have to do but we need to evolve an overall strategy. First, we need to leverage the global opportunity and create an economic momentum, the inflow of money momentum to drive growth. At the same time, it is impractical to just meet the needs of 10 million or 20 million people in India's knowledge industry and not have the rest of the country moving. Therefore, we have to use strategic momentum and leverage we are getting from all the things that Mukesh talked about and marry that to the other set of initiatives that ensures that the broad fruits of this economic momentum are much more equitable. That is the only way we are going to get sustainability in a political sense to achieve what we want.

Our research laboratories are the fountainhead of new ideas change in order to partake in the global community and

To me, infrastructure is a means to an end, in the sense that it is not a big deal to build an airport or a road. We can always hire people to get that done. But the governance model has to be dramatically improved. Let me give you three instances in India in the last twenty years where there has been a dramatic transformation – all of it really leveraging the power of modern technology.

Take, first, our financial systems. In the mid 80s when the financial system was reformed and Dr Rangarajan[5] came out with his first report on bank computerisation, the prevailing climate of opinion was such that you could not even use the word computerisation. If you remember this report, it was called 'mechanisation' because computerisation was a red flag. Now, from that stage and because of all the reforms brought in by private banks, today we have one of the world's most advanced financial infrastructures. We have complete paperless trading, electronic stock exchanges, the dematerialisation of our stocks, banks running online real-time systems and real-time gross settlement systems with

5 Dr C. Rangarajan, Former Reserve Bank of India Governor and Member of the Economic Advisory Council to the Prime Minister, 1985-91.

the Reserve Bank. We suddenly have a financial infrastructure that is better than the one in the US because we were able to marry our innate capability with technology. We have a tax information system which rides on top of this network. Build the scaffolding and the infrastructure, and you can actually leapfrog on that.

My second example is the elections and the fact that we could conduct an election with 1.7 million electronic voting machines. We seen the kind of issues with elections elsewhere and, therefore, in one step we leapfrogged and used technology to do that.

The third example is what Mukesh and his colleagues have done. They are on the verge of ensuring that every nook and cranny of this country is accessible using the Internet. This has all been done in a matter of years.

and that is where we would like to see a huge attitudnal global business. – Kiran Mazumdar-Shaw

What these mean is that if you have the opportunities and trends in technology, you can marry the two and create competitive leapfrogging advantages that you could not do earlier.

If we apply the same concept to governance – marry governance to technological change – then suddenly from seeing democracy as a drag, it will become our source of competitive advantage and an instrument by which we can grow faster in a more equitable way.

N.K. Singh: Thanks Nandan, that's quite a mindset change. Subir, would you like to add to what the three panellists have said – Mukesh clearly focusing on human resource development; Kiran still talking in terms of the greatest synergy and Nandan emphasising very clearly a governance model which will give some of the other areas the kind of synergy that is required.

Subir Raha: More than representing the so-called old economy, let me speak as a citizen of this country. Which India are we talking about? According to statistics, in 1990 there were some 790 million people in Asia who lived on less than $1 a day. This number dropped to something, if I remember, 350 or 450 million by 2002 and 75 per cent of this decline happened in China.

So which India are we talking about? We have great professional skills and great high education. This is true but the 'can-do' attitude, which I fully agree with Kiran, is primarily due to the reach of global television. The rise in aspiration is remarkable. We are no longer resigned to our fate. People are looking for a bright future. They are willing to work for that future. The issue is: how do we create the opportunity to leverage this change of attitude?

Thanks to communication – whether it is visual communication on television or the Internet or telephone services – we are interlinked and, therefore, it is just not possible to pull off bluffs on the population anymore. We have a great opportunity of actual change, the issue is the solution which has been suggested.

Governance is a very generic word. Perhaps one good starting point is that while we have done very well in high education we need to focus on education across the population. We need to make sure that we have these huge human resources and the development of that in terms of secondary education and vocational education actually takes place and we get away from a situation where a large majority of our population lives on less than $1 a day.

N.K. Singh: So, in addition to the challenges of human resource development, the governance model which Nandan emphasised, Subir would like to ensure that the technology divides does not lead to greater inequalities and that is the third challenge which the panellists would like to introduce. Would you, Kiran, like to respond?

Kiran Mazumdar-Shaw: In the process of India achieving a faster rate of economic growth this technology divide and accentuation of income divides is one area which can be avoided in the policy framework.

But I want to also add another dimension and that is the healthcare challenge. Subir has raised an important point: there are two Indias and we have to reach out to the other India wherein the healthcare challenge that we have is enormous and the disease burden is enormous. It is technology and a sort of convergence of technologies which will actually help us address these challenges.

We are looking at various models and mechanisms for low-cost health insurance and all this is going to be possible through biotechnology, our home grown pharmaceutical industry and generic drugs with, of course, information technology playing a very important role in networking all kinds of medical resources. What we really have to provide is a very affordable healthcare system.

N.K. Singh: Thanks Kiran for introducing the health challenge as another important priority area which is of concern. But Nandan, would you like to specifically comment on what the country can do to ensure the fruits of economic growth do not really lead to an accentuation of income and digital divides and what kind of a policy framework would ensure that?

Nandan Nilekani: The question is how to create jobs for everybody because if you do that, the rest takes care of itself. Jobs will create people with incomes, and those who have purchasing power will buy things and, therefore, lead to a growth in GDP.

We cannot expect that the knowledge industry will create jobs for everybody. Partly because there may not be that many jobs and partly because people may not have educational and skill levels to participate. But there are lots of other sectors which will create jobs. For example, agriculture. Today, what is happening in the West is that there is a huge amount of subsidies that farmers get. It is quite high, much higher than the spending on science and research and development and this is an historical thing even though only 2 to 3 per cent of their economy is on agricultural subsidies.

Over the next few years as the populations age in these countries, what is called the dependency ratio is going to go up. This means that the number of old people who will rely on the number of young people will go up. There will be pension costs, healthcare costs and they won't be able to afford these subsidies anymore.

Therefore agriculture globally is going to open up over the next ten to fifteen years. It is clearly a huge play for us.

The second thing that is opening up on the WTO is the garment side by 2005. This will enable us to double or triple our garment exports substantially. Why I am saying this is because each of these are different engines of job creation. We can create jobs in the garment industry; we can create jobs in agriculture. I think we have to have a multifaceted job engine creation philosophy where there are at least eight to ten engines of job creation that we work on which will address different parts of the population and different regions in the country.

If we can spread this economic activity and job creation across the country and different sectors, you will make it far more equitable.

N.K. Singh: Thanks Nandan for responding to that question. Of course, in India it is only after 2040 that you will find the dependency ratio really increasing. Between now and 2040, there's a kind of window of opportunity that Mukesh was talking about. But Mukesh do you have any further observation to make on the issue of digital divide or the income divide and what can be done to really ensure that technology development and growth does not really further accentuate this tension?

Mukesh Ambani: I have a couple of very simple points to make. I believe that in the next two or three decades, technology will be the biggest leveller. Technology is going to equate all human beings, and that opportunity is real. Ever since the discovery of the phone, in the last hundred years we have not been able to cover all of India. In the next ten years, I can assure you, this divide will be eliminated. Take this beyond communications to the next generation health products that will be available: new health delivery systems, new education delivery systems, and other all kinds of delivery systems.

We've seen the failure of Communism: that's the learning of the past fifty years. If you try to distribute income without first fundamentally focusing on creating wealth then it's not going to work.

India needs to be very focused in terms of making sure we create wealth – and I respect Nandan's industry for showing us the way. He is a little defensive in terms of this business of equitably distributing it, but I think you first need to create wealth. Once you have created wealth then you automatically start a cycle: twenty million people earning $4 trillion. This $4 trillion circulates in the Indian economy and creates secondary, tertiary jobs. It's going to have India fired on all counts. It is going to fire agriculture. It is going to fire complex manufacturing. It is going to fire research. And that is when we will become a very vibrant domestic market.

The big opportunity is to make India one of the biggest

consumption markets in the world in the next twenty to thirty years. That alone is a huge opportunity and can protect us from huge income divides and disparities.

Disparity is a way of life. It exists even in the US. What we should work towards is to reduce this 1:100 disparity to 1:10 and then bring it down. Directionally we must be focused on wealth creation first and then put in a methodology of distribution. We must ensure we first have access to capital from the world which can then be used to multiply within India.

N.K. Singh: Okay, Mukesh that's one point of view. I don't want to open this unsettled area of economic controversy of whether growth and wealth creation automatically translate into income distribution patterns which would be, in some way, equitable and rational.

How do you really ensure that wealth creation does not skew incomes but ensures that the fruits of wealth are more evenly divided? Nandan you seem to have a slight variant on that and, therefore, would you like to respond to Mukesh?

Nandan Nilekani: I do not want to get into a debate with Mukesh but I am completely with him on wealth creation. This is what I've been doing for twenty-five years. But the point is this we have to win in five years. I cannot tell my young friends to wait for twenty years. It is not going to work that way. Everybody wants to know what's in it for them. While we have to support wealth creation and make sure that we tie into the global opportunity, we have to have a parallel track of rapidly expediting opportunities for everybody else. We have to bind everyone to this vision to get political sustainability and get this game going, otherwise it's going to happen only in fits and starts.

Kiran Mazumdar-Shaw: I believe that technology is going to be a leveller and we are going to have a multiplier effect based on various initiatives, including infrastructure. Infrastructure itself is going to bring about a lot of connectivity into the hinterland which will bring up economic growth and opportunities so that the rest of India can also partake in the economic boom that we expect.

Moderator | **N.K. Singh**

Member, Planning Commission

Gautam Nath: Why don't we apply corporate governance standards to bureaucrats and politicians? For example, for bureaucrats, we could have pay for performance, performance improvement plans and quality performance reviews. In industry, people retire at 62 years of age. We could apply that to politicians. We have had the BJP losing power, which means the product it sold was not accepted. Shouldn't Vajpayee, CEO Advani and CEO Mahajan leave politics forever.

Nandan Nilekani: Well, politics is more competitive than business. What you are talking about is bringing market concepts into governance. At the end of the day, all of us – Mukesh, myself and Kiran – have shareholders and are answerable to them. There is a high level of information transparency. Every quarter we give our results and if our shareholders believe that our performance is not up to par, they can replace us with other managers.

The same thing happens in politics but on a much longer, five-year, timeframe. However, if you can bring the same level of information transparency into the governance models and if you can create institutional frameworks for sharing that information with the people, then you will create the equivalent of what you said. Once you do that, accountability and transparency will go up; people's expectations will go up and you will be able to identify who is performing and who is not in a much shorter timeframe. Quality of outcomes will automatically improve.

N.K. Singh: Subir, you are the only one who is, technically, representing the government. Would you have any comment to add to what Nandan has suggested?

Subir Raha: The question was on corporate governance and, as

Nandan pointed out, disclosure requirements are perhaps the single most important element in corporate governance procedures. Therefore, if we take advantage of electronics, which has lowered the bar of literacy, and use that for freedom of information in the governance and bureaucratic system and bring the same regard of disclosure, we will solve half the problems.

The essential tendency is to hold things back or hold them within a small group of people, however, enlightened they may be. The desirable thing would be to implement disclosure norms – whether you are in a corporate boardroom or in a governed ministry.

Scott Bayman (President and CEO, GE-India): If there were two things that the government could either do, or undo, to facilitate the opportunities that all of you have addressed today what would they be?

Mukesh Ambani: Government must empower our already strong public sector. It is critical that governments and ministers get out of the dilemma that this is my company this is multinational's, this is the Indian private sector's and so on. It is a government's job to treat all equally. The public sectors in India is very vibrant and strong. It really needs to be unleashed to compete globally. The first thing is to let the force of the public sector – the strong public sector – perform on an independent basis.

The second is to leapfrog our governance systems. Just as industry has changed and moved away from manufacturing, finance and marketing to an integrated whole, government must have competitive systems so that it consciously stays out of the business of business. I think India has an opportunity to do that, and we can drastically reinvent and re-engineer our day-to-day management systems.

Nandan Nilekani: Clearly, we have to take governance to new levels and also infrastructure has to be world class. The problem is not that we don't have the money. There is enough money floating around to get things done. Nor is it a question of execution capability – Mukesh can roll out a telecom network within two years, he can build a world-class plant in Jamnagar in 18 months, Infosys is building 3.5 million square feet of office space in the next few months – so, we can do it. It's not such a big deal.

There really are multiple issues at play. One, is the financing model but there are other issues of ownership, of land. Take one example which I am reasonably familiar with – Bangalore International Airport which has been pending for decades. It has nothing to do with our ability to build an airport – anybody can build an airport – it costs half a million dollars and we can raise the money in one day.

But the bottlenecks are to do with other influences – peoples' interests and motives. That's the far bigger problem to solve than the mechanistic, technocratic problem. It is really to do with ownership, governance and accountability.

N. K. Singh: Is there a specific suggestion on whether public/private partnership could be made faster to improve the quality of project implementation?

Nandan Nilekani: There are number of things that public/ private partnerships can do. First, is to bring in a sort of social venture capital into the business that allows you try to out new things which you can't do in a historical government-financing network.

Second, it allows you to bring in an intellectual and project mandate with best practices into the way you do things. And third, you can import ideas of accountability from the private sector into the public sector. You won't have institutional mechanisms but, at least, you can create make shift mechanisms to create some kind of accountability.

Phiroz Vandrewala (Executive Vice President, Tata Consultancy Services): We've been talking about governance, but what is the reality on the ground? Is anything going to change in the next five to ten years? We're going to have regional politicians and coalition governments, You're going to have Uttar Pradesh and Bihar – fifteen years have not changed anything so I don't see things changing in the next five or ten years. We need to focus on the ground realities.

Mukesh Ambani: Well, I think the problem is also to do with instant gratification. All over the world, and younger people in India too, want instant gratification. There is no simple answer, but I can see very dramatic changes in the last twenty three or twenty four years in the economy. In the last twenty years, from my point of view, things have changed – and the biggest change is that with coalition politics who is in power and who isn't does not affect us. That's a very big mindset change for business. It's like saying politicians can get on with law and order and leave the economy alone.

Manzar Khan (Sports Management Group International, London): Mr Ambani, we hear a lot about the Tatas in social areas and we've heard about your megaprojects in India and abroad. But I personally have not heard much about your social projects. You've spoken about education leading to sustainable development but are you undertaking such projects?

Mukesh Ambani: I would not like to use this forum as a publicity forum for Reliance. What I can tell you is that in education, health and rural development there is a lot of involvement of the top 30 or 40 corporates. There is involvement at the ground level, in terms of technology and delivering technology to the masses and in making sure that there is an education and health delivery system.

A lot of industries are involved in disaster management, particularly after the earthquake in Gujarat. A lot of industries are involved with the security infrastructure of a lot of cities on a pilot basis. We have industry/government partnership in terms of making sure that we work together and that the authorities are able to use our skills and competencies to deliver more and more value to millions of citizens. And Reliance, of course, is very much a part of that.

Prem Shankar Jha (Senior Journalist): I have very one brief observation for Mr. Raha and a question for all the panelists. Mr Raha with reference to the BRIC's report you mentioned, I am really troubled about how much we have lost in the last forty years as well as the great 7.5 per cent possibility for the next forty years. I think both the loss and the potential gain are exaggerated because one of the problems with this report is that it ignores the political affect on economic development.

In the last forty years we have had slow growth because of excessive centralisation but it also gave us time to build national unity. It is because of this that today it is possible for 60 to 80 million Indians to work outside their home states without there being any kind of backlash.

My question is that given that in the future we cannot go on, for example, with the present situation in Bihar with 2.2 per cent per capita growth, in Maharashtra it is plus 5 per cent and in Gujarat it is plus 7 per cent and that the state is going to have to intervene to look after the losers. Now as major decision makers who have changed the face of India how much can you do on your own?

Subir Raha: Your point on the BRICs report is well taken. We know that every forecast is based on certain assumptions and data and, therefore, all forecasts are open to challenge, based on those assumptions. The point which I was really making is that regardless of whether it is 7.5 or 4.5 or 'x' per cent, we have not used the opportunity that we had over the years.

You talked about national unity. Certainly we have done tremendous things in the last fifty-seven years but when it comes to the national unity, let me submit to you two examples. Perhaps the country was never more united than when we lost the war in 1962; perhaps the country was never more united than when we won the war in 1971 yet in the last year we had a situation where the employment of gangmen in the Railways led to riots in four states.

It is true that we have made tremendous progress in communications, IT and agriculture – and we must be proud of what we have achieved. At the same time, let us not get bogged down by particulars of statistics. We should have done even better and without shedding tears on what we could not do or have not done, we need to think about what we are going to do in the next few years and how we will build on what we have achieved.

N. K. Singh: Prem's second question is the classic unresolved question of growth versus equity. While fostering economic growth, what are some of the tangibles that can be done and should be done to make sure that certain people left behind in the growth process really do not become drags on that growth?

Mukesh Ambani: As far as taking care of the vulnerable class of our people, we have got to have governance to make sure that the most vulnerable are protected to a certain basic quality of life. What India will have in each of its 640,000 villages by the end of 2005 is a next generation technology infrastructure whereby we can communicate and transact with our billion people.

The real thing we can do is to use the technology and the technology infrastructure to ensure that our subsidies and money earmarked in our State and Central budgets, which is not reaching the people it is intended for, gets to those who deserve it. A case in point is LPG. There is no need for Mukesh Ambani or Nandan Nilekani to be subsidised for LPG at Rs. x a cylinder. We should pay market price for LPG but people who cannot afford that cooking gas should be directly given that subsidy. Technology will enable that and that is a concrete thing we can do.

Jyotiraditya Scindia (Member of Parliament, Congress): My question is related to the issue of employment generation. A comment was made with regard to high growth and productivity without necessarily increasing the employment generation potential in our country. Over the last five or six years even though we have had 4.5 to 5.5 per cent growth and an increase in productivity, employment generation has actually fallen.

Related to that is the issue of the break up of GDP. If you look at manufacturing versus services you have 26 per cent in manufacturing and 50 per cent in services which is the exact converse of China. Software and services are being made out to be a panacea to all ills plaguing the economy today and in a lot of ways, people are content with the notion that we have leapfrogged the manufacturing revolution straight to the software generation.

Isn't there also a danger that China will catch up on the services front as well? Should we ignore the manufacturing sector at our own peril? Manufacturing sectors have fallen from 12 per cent growth rate to almost 6 per cent today. Isn't that something we should look at seriously, instead of highlighting and spotlighting the software sector?

Nandan Nilekani: Rather than just look at manufacturing versus service, we have to look at the labour intensity of an activity and focus on those things that have strategic leverage and labour intensity. For example, you say manufacturing, but if I invest $5 billion in a silicon foundry, I will create only 100 jobs. So there isn't a direct correlation that manufacturing leads to jobs and services does not mean just software because even the guy who drives a truck and carries agricultural produce from villages to cities is providing a service.

We need to think out-of-the-box about labour intensive activities. For example, garments, where you need nimble hands to cut and sew, is a labour intensive activity and that alone can create million of jobs in the next five years. Similarly, the entire supply chain of moving products from farms and factories to consumers creates jobs. What we need to do is look at labour intensity across a spectrum of activities and focus on creating multiplier effects.

Subir Raha: I agree with Mr Scindia's observation. I would like to submit two things for consideration: one, we've had a very closed economy with tremendous amount of production. Both the public and private sectors built capacities in the 1950s, '60s, '70s, '80s. But it was only when production had been diluted that investments in building manufacturing capacity slowed down, except for a few exceptions.

There is no new investment coming in because as entrepreneurs we are not willing to invest in technology and take on competition, this is the hard fact of the manufacturing world. Today, what we are looking back on is the debris of a huge amount of capacity created from the 1950s to the 1980s – but replacing the debris with new technology and new capacities is perhaps something Parliament and the government should agitate on. Our policy framework is not encouraging to building new capacities in the country.

Mukesh Ambani: I would like to say that for any economy the key is, as Mr Scindia said, to have a strategy to create jobs and the strategy to create jobs really depends on two factors: one is the purchasing power in the economy – and inflow of capital is very important for that purchasing power. Two is the skill level of all participants so that they can, on a competitive basis, deliver value.

If we look at job creation – and I will give you an example of Reliance Infocomm that for the 10 million new subscribers that we created, we created a total of 150,000 new jobs across the value chain. So, if India moves from 10 million to 100 million subscribers, you are creating 1.5 million new jobs and these are at different levels of competencies because the purchasing power of buying and paying for a phone at Rs 200 a month exists.

> It is particularly important that huge and populous countries like India and China, which are rapidly expanding their energy use, develop the nuclear option and do so with full regard for the requirements of safe operations and safe waste disposal.

Preventing Nuclear Weapons **From Falling into the** Hands of Rogue States and Terrorists

Dr Hans Blix

Dr Hans Blix

Former Head, UN Monitoring Verification and Inspection Commission for Iraq

Plucked out of retirement by UN Secretary General Kofi Annan to head the UN Monitoring, Verification and Inspection Commission (UNMOVIC), Hans Blix was handed the difficult job of verifying Iraq's compliance with disarmament promises made after the 1991 Gulf War.

Placed in the global spotlight, Blix had to handle delicate negotiations with the Iraqis on the one side and the allied forces, primarily the US and the UK, on the other. A seasoned diplomat with knowledge of international law and jurisprudence and, most importantly, an unflappable style that won him friends and admirers throughout the Middle East he was the right man for the job.

Born in Uppsala, Sweden in 1928, Blix received a PhD from Cambridge University in England. He earned a doctorate in law from Stockholm University in 1959, where he also served as a professor of international law.

From 1963 to 1976, Blix served in the Swedish Foreign Ministry and in 1978 became that country's Minister for Foreign Affairs. From 1962 to 1978, he was a member of the Swedish delegation to the Conference on Disarmament in Geneva, Switzerland. He was also a member of Sweden's delegation to the UN General Assembly for twenty years, from 1961 until 1981. From 1981 until 1997, he served as Director General of the International Atomic Energy Agency (IAEA).

Blix has largely been a critic of the invasion of Iraq, steadfastly maintaining that the case for war by the US and the UK was 'over interpreted' as well of the manner in which the allied forces bypassed the UN.

His book, *Disarming Iraq: The Search for Weapons of Mass Destruction,* documents his experiences and the events that led to the 2003 Gulf War.

Blix is currently the head of an independent commission on Weapons of Mass Destruction.

I WOULD TAKE THIS OPPORTUNITY TO DISCUSS THE BURNING ISSUE OF NUCLEAR WEAPONS IN TODAY'S WORLD.

The title given to my comments might seem to suggest that nuclear weapons are now in the hands of prudent and mature states and that we only have to watch out that they do not fall into the hands of some rogues – whoever they may be – or terrorists. I believe our concerns must be little broader than that. Not so many years ago, we agonised – rightly in my view – about the US and the Soviet Union engaging in mutually assured destruction (MAD) and wiping out the rest with human civilisation as collateral damage. The nuclear stockpiles have been reduced since that time, but there is little reason to be complacent about 'any' weapons of mass destruction anywhere.

I am currently heading a fifty-member independent international Commission on Weapons of Mass Destruction (WMD). It is holding its third session next week in Vancouver and will report well after the end of next year. What I will present here, of course, are my personal views, not the commission's.

Let me start by addressing the broad issue of security because the problems of non-proliferation and of reduction and elimination of WMD are almost invariably linked to the perceptions of security.

I will begin on one optimistic and one pessimistic note.

First, the optimistic: I think that humanity has put the era of world wars behind itself.

The pessimistic one is that I am as concerned about the long-term global environmental threats, notably global warming, as I am about the short-term threats of WMD. From time immemorial, the world's peoples and nations have demonstrated their talent for destroying each other. They now seem to join hands and talent to destroy the environment we have adapted to. Fossil fuels, which took the planet millions of years to create, will be burnt up in a few hundred years. It may come to warm us more than we like.

I shall not dwell on the point which is not on the agenda. Let me say only that I am as much in favour of a much-expanded reliance on nuclear power to restrain the use of fossil fuels, as I am in favour of nuclear non-proliferation and disarmament. It is important not only for environmental but also for security reasons. Let us use enriched uranium and plutonium for energy generation and not for weapons – megawatts instead of megatons! It is particularly important that huge and populous countries like India and China, which are rapidly expanding their energy use, develop the nuclear option and do so with full regard for the requirements of safe operations and safe waste disposal. Nuclear power and nuclear weapons are not Siamese twins; states can have nuclear weapons without having nuclear power, but the reverse is possible and far preferable. The atom can be for peace, as US President Eisenhower told us fifty years ago. Needless to say, I also favour a more efficient use of energy and renewable sources.

Let me return to the prospects for world peace. Whether we want it or not, the gradual global integration that is being brought about by the modern, technical, economic and information evolution, I believe, is gluing us together and will push relations between blocs and continents towards peace. The future controversies between the great powers are likely, I think, to play out in the areas of trade and finance rather than on the battlefields.

This optimism one can feel regarding great powers and blocs does not apply to a number of volatile regions. There will certainly also be armed conflicts within states.

The war in Iraq was undertaken, the world was told, precisely to eliminate ready and real WMDs and to eliminate the risk that WMDs be transferred to terrorists. However, while we have witnessed how swift military action by the world's only military superpower removed a murderous leader, we have also witnessed how the counter-proliferations surgery failed simply because there were no WMDs in Iraq. The pre-emptive action was costly in terms of life, money and international relations to make sure that there were no WMDs.

I shall return to the question of pre-emptive armed action a little later, but let me say already at this point that in my view the best chance to contain and solve regional conflicts and the risk of WMD is through international cooperation: through diplomacy and international agreements, international human and economic development and, where appropriate, economic and military pressures.

I am not suggesting that the UN is the only multilateral church in town, but it is also not one to be ignored lightly. Acting through a limited alliance against the will of the majority of the UN Security Council, in the case of Iraq, proved to be a much greater problem than foreseen by those who proclaimed the irrelevance of the UN. One would hope that the next US administration will resume the responsibility of the lead wolf, which it was, and only in truly exceptional circumstances act as the lone wolf.

Having said where I think – and hope – we are going, let me briefly discuss where we are coming from.

As far back as we can see in history, king's and people's quest for territory have been one of the main causes of war. How many armed conflicts have taken place over the Rhine in Europe or over the river Amur in Asia? Ideological aims have been behind many other armed campaigns: the Christian Crusades, colonial campaigns and campaigns for the conversion of people to Christianity or Islamic Jehads against infidels. I think these two main causes of armed conflicts between states are disappearing. Perhaps Saddam Hussein's war against Iran and efforts to seize space in the Shatt-el-Arab and his occupation of Kuwait were amongst the last cases of inter-state aggression for the old fashioned purpose of grabbing territory.

During the many years of the Cold War, the Communist camp sought to expand in the name of ideology. The security system of the UN Charter, which is based on the idea that the Security Council may intervene against breaches of peace and acts of aggression, was, on the whole, inoperative. Any one of the five permanent members could prevent action by casting a veto. The states of the world had to find their security through their own defence, through alliances or neutrality. The great territorial changes that did occur – mostly peacefully – were the emancipation of colonies.

After the end of the Cold War and the collapse of Communism, the security situation has changed drastically in the world. There is continued détente between all big powers and blocs – if, indeed, one can speak of blocs any longer. There are no significant territorial or ideological conflicts between them. All pursue the market economy of various shapes and shades as their economic model. All are bent on pragmatism and none on ideological conquest. Many states in Europe are now reorienting their armed forces from defence of their territory to use in joint international peace-keeping or peace-enforcing operations.

The détente helped to strengthen security globally and in several regions in Africa and Central America, tensions and conflicts disappeared.

During the Cold War, nuclear capability had spread beyond the permanent five of the Security Council to Israel, India, Pakistan and South Africa. After the end of the Cold War, the Ukraine and Kazakhstan transferred their nuclear weapons to Russia and Argentina. Brazil and Algeria committed themselves legally to non-proliferation by joining the Nuclear Non-Proliferation Treaty (NPT). South Africa became the first country to roll back from a nuclear weapon status.

At the United Nations and in international organisations, détente made it possible to achieve many things together which earlier had been impossible. A great many peace-keeping missions were authorised by the Security Council, and the use of the veto became rare. Even after the divisive UN proceedings in the Iraq affair, there were, last year, about fifteen ongoing UN-led peace-keeping missions, comprising some fifty-thousand soldiers costing about $4 billion per year. It does not sound cheap, but it is a bargain compared to war.

The most important UN action made possible by the new climate of détente was, of course, the authorisation given to the broad alliance created by President Bush the elder to intervene in 1991 to stop Iraq's naked aggression against the occupation of Kuwait. For some time that action gave hope to the world that a new will of governments to cooperate would at long last bring the security provisions of the charter to life.

In the field of arms control and the disarmament the global détente brought several welcome results, above all the conclusion of the Chemical Weapons Convention and the Comprehensive Test Ban Treaty (CTBT) and the expectation that agreement would be reached to stop all production of highly enriched uranium and plutonium for more nuclear weapons (FMCT): the so-called cut-offs.

The peace dividends of the early détente were, indeed, great. Many straight-jackets imposed in a bipolar world vanished. In recent years, some have looked back with nostalgia to the stability of the Cold War period and it is true that some lids came off at that time, which perhaps we would have preferred to stay on. But looking at the situation today, I feel nostalgic for the period when détente gave a rich harvest which was in the first part of the 1990s.

Paradoxically, while the détente between the great powers has remained, the positive evolution seems to have gone.

Not so long ago, President Bush declared that 9/11 was the Pearl Harbour of World War III and Vice President Cheney said that the war against terrorism could last for generations and require the US to have military bases all over the world. A recent news article even specified where such future bases were to be placed in Iraq.

A full-page article in the *Financial Times* in August of this year by Mr Bolton, Under-Secretary for Arms Control and International Security in the US State Department, looked like another straw in the post-détente wind. Mr Bolton described how 'robust' cooperation between the US and its allies rather than reliance on what he termed 'cumbersome treaty-based bureaucracies' can produce 'real results'.

Mr Bolton did not discuss how successful such alliance-cooperation was in 2002 and 2003 to identify WMD in Iraq, nor how alliance-intelligence compared with the reports of cumbersome international bureaucracies – the inspectors of the UN system. Rather, he extolled various arrangements initiated by the US, like the Proliferation Security Initiative (PSI) and the securing of nuclear material and equipment because these are 'activities' not organisations.

How are we to understand this apparent allergy to precise treaty commitments which was also visible in the latest nuclear verification free US disarmament accord with Russia?

Is it a new attitude prompted by a wish to shake off any external restraints and to retain full freedom of action together with those who, in any given case, are 'with us' and ignore those who are 'against us'? If so, one would hope that the Iraq war should give some food for thought.

Today, we seem to be at a post 9/11 and post Iraq war fork of the road.

The US agenda had emphasised counter-proliferation, confrontation and pre-emption, if need be, through unilateral military action. Although use of international organisations like the UN or the IAEA (International Atomic Energy Agency), has continued, the reliance on and cooperation through formal treaty alliances, instruments and agreements seems to have been de-emphasised. The agenda followed seems to have emerged from the feeling that the US military power is so great that time consuming and tedious talk in international fora can be dispensed with. Activity, not agreement, has been seen as important.

Where are we going next? I shall first discuss the WMD threats linked to terrorist groups and thereafter the treats from WMD in the hands of states.

The first point to make, I think, is that terrorists do not live on clouds, but must have their feet on the territory of states. It is important that the international community upholds the principle that each government is obliged to ensure that its territory is not used as a base for attacks against other states. It is legally correct and practically and politically sound. If there is a failure in this duty, then the world will endorse forcible intervention – as it did with the Taliban government in Afghanistan.

Second, the broad international efforts described by Mr Bolton to ensure the safe keeping of nuclear and other dangerous material and equipment everywhere in the world are important to reduce the availability of such material and equipment. If the Pakistan government had exercised better control of its nuclear sector, Mr Khan's shop for nuclear designs and centrifuges would not have been in this dangerous business.

Most of the measures, which governments need to take to reduce the risk of terrorists wielding 'dirty bombs', biological or chemical weapon are needed also to protect their own public against radiation, the release of bacteria or viruses or the dangers of various chemicals. There is much international cooperation in the field of radiation protection and in the prevention of trafficking in nuclear material and equipment. Similar efforts could be undertaken in the biological field, for instance, the elaboration of model legislation and model administrative routines. The World Health Organization (WHO) as well as individual states could be of help.

Third, what is mostly needed immediately is intensified international cooperation in the day-to-day fieldwork of the national intelligence, police and financial institutions of states to trace persons, resources, weapons and dangerous material. There seems to be a somewhat futile debate whether the combating of terrorism is a task for law enforcement organisations or the military. In most cases using military means would be like deploying cannons against mosquitoes.

This is not to deny that military operations may be inevitable to crush or flush out armed terrorist units, where they have been identified as based in a particular area, for instance, in parts of Afghanistan or Pakistan. Such operations need to be based on reliable evidence. After the Al-Qaeda inspired attacks on the US embassies in Nairobi and Dar-es-Salaam, the Clinton administration sent cruise missiles to a chemical factory, which was located outside Khartoum and which had been erroneously identified as linked to Al-Qaeda. Such military actions – whether for the purpose of punishment or counter-proliferation – are unacceptable. They cannot be just shrugged off.

One of the purposes claimed for the military invasion of Iraq was to prevent the promotion of Al-Qaeda and other terrorist groups, allegedly supported by Iraq. If this was really an aim, it was one that failed singularly. It is evident that the occupation has prompted and stimulated terrorism and that harsh and illegal response measures, in this case as in similar cases – at Abu Ghraib and Guantanamo as in Chechnya – breed further terrorism and risks driving large numbers of civilians, otherwise not favourable to the extremist, to support them.

Although there is not much basis for the alarm about a 'war of civilisations', it is bad enough if the struggle against Islamic Jehadists were to be pursued in such a way as to further strengthen anti-American and anti-western attitudes amongst the vast number of Islamic moderates and vice versa. It would then stimulate the very terrorism it seeks to stop.

The Prime Minister of India talks about the 'confluence of civilizations' rather than a clash and I think it is a good idea to have that picture before us.

After 9/11 or after a Beslan massacre the mood is simply to punish the perpetrators and to eradicate the responsible group. Yet, for a longer term, it is rational to ask why the terrorists commit such atrocities. To be sure, their motives vary and many will be muddled or absurd. However, if reasonable non-armed measures can be taken, which reduce incentives to terrorism, they should be on the agenda, whether they are in the fields of economic or social development or greater autonomy for particular groups or regions. It is not pandering to terrorism but simply rational.

It was refreshing to hear Tony Blair recently saying that nothing would be more important to reduce terrorism in the Middle East than a solution to the Israeli-Palestinian problem and that he would devote himself to this issue.

Even though there is concern that terrorist groups may get hold of and employ nuclear weapons, the concern is much more acute and indicated by recent experience about nuclear weapons in the hands of states. I mentioned the success cases of Ukraine,

Kazakhstan and South Africa. Regrettably the story is not complete without a mention also of the de facto proliferation to the non-NPT parties – Israel, India and Pakistan, the attempted violations by the (NPT-parties) North Korea (DPRK), Iraq and Libya and a suspected but denied violation by Iran, which is also a party to the NPT.

How should the world community tackle these questions?

It is Iran and DPRK that today make us hold our breath and that raise a host of difficult questions and fears of domino effects should either acquire or deploy nuclear weapons.

Both countries have acted in disregard of their safeguard obligation. DPRK, which has renounced the NPT, has claimed that it is ready to deter foreign attacks by developing a nuclear weapon capacity, but it has also declared that it is ready to 'scrap' such a capacity if some conditions are fulfilled, including guarantees about security from attack. Iran has declared that its intention is only to use its legal right under the NPT to enrich uranium in order to make fuel for its own power reactors. It has also signalled that while it cannot accept being deprived of this right, it might consider voluntarily suspending some activities, including enrichment, if the quid pro quo was sufficient.

In both cases a number of states are, at present, seeking solutions through negotiations. This is welcome. The war that was waged in Iraq is not a model that many would want to see followed.

Solutions for DPRK and Iran must aim at ensuring that both states renounce all nuclear activities though bomb grade material could be produced and accept far-reaching verification. The minimum in this regard would be full acceptance of the additional safeguards agreements of the IAEA. To induce them to make such commitments will require some attractive quid pro quo in both cases.

As regards DPRK, I submit it might be wise to make the economic part of the package attractive by construing it in a way that would help the country gradually to exit from the system that has brought it to misery and starvation.

The economic part of an agreement with Iran will need to cover trade and investment relations, perhaps support for WTO membership. Such chips seem, indeed, to be among the European proposals. If Iran is to forego the investments it has made in infrastructure for an indigenous production of enriched uranium for use in power reactors, a multilateral assurance of supply of uranium fuel at market prices for the country's power reactors – and more – must evidently be given and seems, indeed, to be on the negotiating table.

It is my belief that both in the case of Iran and the case of DPRK some guarantees may need to be given about security against attacks from the outside. The DPRK has talked explicitly about a 'non-aggression pact', which sounds a little something out of the Stalinist period, but the substance is more important than the form. It is encouraging that there seems also to have been some positive responses from the US side.

The potential consequences of DPRK and/or Iran acquiring nuclear weapons are very serious. Let me focus on the case of Iran and say first that in my view it is not surprising that many countries in the world have suspected Iran of intending to move to nuclear weapon – or at least to a near nuclear weapon – status. Iran built infrastructure for the enrichment of uranium disregarding the need for transparency and disregarding express obligations under its safeguards agreement with the IAEA. Although Iran assures the world that it intends to enrich uranium only to the level needed for its own power reactor fuel, it could later go to a concentration needed for weapons. Iran has further engaged in building a large heavy water reactor and plants to produce the heavy water needed. This type of reactor is deemed convenient for the production of plutonium, provided that a reprocessing capacity is available, which does not seem to be the case at the present – at least not on an industrial scale.

This is not, however, the full picture. It has been said by some critics that there is no justification for Iran as an oil rich country to build nuclear power plants. This, I think, is almost a colonialist argument. Why should an oil rich country not produce electricity by nuclear power and sell the oil it thereby saves for good income in the world market? The argument was never advanced when the Shah was still in Iran and the US and other states competed with each other to sell nuclear infrastructure to the country.

It might be said with more reason that building an indigenous enrichment capacity to produce nuclear fuel for a few reactors is not necessary and might not be economic. My own country, Sweden has eleven nuclear power reactors generating around ten thousand megawatt and does not enrich the fuels it needs but buys it in the world market. It might be more economic. At the same time, it must be admitted, it makes for dependence on outside suppliers. In a free world market this might not matter much but the reality is that the government of Iran has had a painful experience in this field of assurance of supply a number of years ago, when it needed fresh enriched uranium fuel for its Teheran-based research reactor.

It must be added that Iran is right in saying the NPT does not prohibit it from enriching uranium – only from making nuclear weapons. This should be recognised. Indeed, three other non-nuclear weapon state parties to the NPT, Brazil, Japan and South Africa, have enrichment capacity, without any international objection being raised. Nor does the NPT bar the construction of a heavy water research reactor. Hence, when it is urged – wisely in my view – that Iran should refrain from all activities, even though per se legal, which may bring it closer to a capacity to make weapons usable material, Iran can ask for something in return. How much? Here we are in the diplomatic bazaar you might say.

US representatives seem to consider it evident that Iran has been, and keeps moving to, a nuclear weapon status and urge the matter to be referred by the Board of Governors of the IAEA to the Security Council. In the speech to the American Enterprise Institute in Washington, Mr Bolton is reported to have said that the agency is required to refer cases to the Security Council once 'questions arise' in connection with compliance and that 'moving the Iran question to the Security Council should be a matter of the smooth functioning of the IAEA system.'

I am not sure that I fully understand what this means. There has been a common assumption in media comments that the US wanted the matter referred to the Council to propose some kind of sanctions. However, considering that China and Russia and others as well may not – at least not yet – be inclined to conclude that Iran has, in effect, so far violated the NPT or is simply temporising, one might wonder what would be the prospects of a proposal for sanctions in the Security Council. Perhaps the aim to move the matter there is different. In the remarkable and forward looking presidential statement from the Security Council summit in 1992, also endorsed by India, which at the time was the member of the council, it was stated that: "The proliferation of all weapons of mass destruction constitutes a threat to international peace and security."

After a reference to the importance of the NPT, effective safeguards and effective export controls, the statement continued: "The members of the Council will take appropriate measures in the case of any violations notified to them by the IAEA."

It may be asked whether it is this responsibility attributed to members – rather than sanctions, decided by the council – that would be the aim of a reference of the Iran issue to the Security Council.

Interestingly, on the other side, the Iranian Parliament, is reported by the BBC recently to have passed the first stage of a bill, which would force the government to resume its uranium enrichment programme. Some parliamentarians were reported as saying that this would, 'strengthen the hands of Iran's negotiators'.

It would seem that the diplomatic game is on – which is better than seeing it off. Newspaper speculations about the bombing of Iranian installations and about Iranian retaliation are added features in the game. The bargaining goes on. But time is running. Let us hope that all sides feel the seriousness of the situation. For Iran, the eradication of Iraq's nuclear programmes must have been an important and positive matter. As we have recently heard from the head of the US appointed Iraq Survey Group Mr Duelfer, Iraq's development of WMD, including nuclear, was aimed primarily at Iran and not at the US.

Under UN Security Council resolution 687 (1991), after the Gulf War, the eradication of Iraq's WMDs and the following long-term monitoring were meant to be steps toward a zone free of WMDs in the Middle East. It is clear that such a zone cannot be negotiated in a time of high tension, but I cannot help wondering whether the Iranian nuclear dimension does not add a further stark reason for new dynamic efforts to ease the central Israeli-Palestinian question. A new initiative could, and should, start all the states in the region on a path away from arms races, dangerous to all of them, to a zone of cooperation free from all WMDs.

This brings me back to the fork in the road, which the world has followed until recently to eliminate WMDs

I confess I see dangers on the road travelled in the last few years by the US administration. Further exploration of new types of American nuclear weapons will not, I think, induce others to disarm and to renounce weapons options that are technically open to them. There maybe more weapons and conflicts, rather than less, on this road.

By contract, a resumption of the kind of leadership that the US used to exercise in the arms control and disarmament fields would, I think, be greeted with enthusiasm by the whole world and could lead all away from WMDs and towards greater security.

In such efforts more attention should be devoted to solving the political, security and social problems that almost invariably underlie the development or acquisition of WMDs.

The US ratification of a comprehensive test ban treaty would likely to have a positive domino effect, including China, India, Pakistan, Iran, Israel and Iraq. It would make the development of new types of nuclear weapons much more difficult.

The conclusion of a verified cut off of the production of fissionable material for weapons combined with agreements on reductions in the number of weapons would gradually reduce the deadly arsenals.

A greater reliance on independent and professional international inspection with broad rights to access on the ground and with some intelligence supplied by national authorities, would give governments, governing boards and the Security Council unbiased assessments. UNMOVIC, which I headed, might be given further functions by the Security Council in the council's proposed stronger engagement to counter WMDs. For instance, as a subsidiary body of the council perhaps it could perform challenge inspections in the fields of biological weapons and missiles, where no inspection mechanisms exist.

In foreign affairs, as in medicine, successful operations required correct diagnoses. They must be directed to real reality – not virtual reality.

Moderator | **Brahma Chellaney**

Professor, Security Studies,
Centre for Policy Research

Kanwar Khalid Younis (Member of Parliament, MQM, Pakistan): There is a theory of deterrence amongst nuclear states, for example, what existed between the US and the USSR in the early fifties, sixties, seventies and eighties. The question is do you also believe that a similar theory could exist or be sustainable between other nuclear states?

Hans Blix: Well, the question on whether mutually assured destruction will work in other cases, I don't think I can be sure of it. If at all it worked between the US and the USSR, it could be also part luck. There were many situations in which at least the US we know seriously contemplated using it and then wisely turned it off. I would not be very comfortable with it.

Q. You referred to a proposal to use inducements to wean Iran away from the process of uranium enrichment. Do you not think it is a bit too late in the day to talk Iran out of its commitment for uranium enrichment? My second question, as you referred to Pakistan's proliferation, there is some indication that A.Q. Khan not only provided technology to North Korea, Libya and Iran but, perhaps, also to a fourth country. Would you like to speculate on which this fourth country could be and what kind of programme would you recommend as an inducement to that country?

Hans Blix: Well, South Africa had the nuclear bomb and they walked away from it. So, it was evidently not too late in that case. I don't think that anything is ever too late, provided the conditions are right.

My assumption is that Iran was looking at its security situation when it moved in this direction – and if those security concerns can be laid to rest and, if moreover, they get other compensations for a voluntary abstention, I don't think it should be too late. It is conceivable that they are just temporising, playing for time. I don't exclude that. But my impression is that they are open to negotiation.

Amrit Kiran Singh (Area Director, Brown Forman): I recently went through the newspapers in Dubai and would it seem that the Islamic world is bending over backward to welcome Mr Bush back to power. I also read a report that the Syrian government has asked the Islamic movement there to stop criticizing the US invasion of Iraq. We have also seen Libya reform and say that it is giving up its nuclear weapons programme. So, perhaps Bush's approach seems to be making progress. The US has got Pakistan, Afghanistan, Iraq, Libya, the whole Islamic world except Iran and may be Syria in the bag.

Hans Blix: On the Islamic countries being in the US bag, well, I don't think the streets of Islamic countries are in the US bag. On the contrary, it seems that the Iraqi affair has brought a great deal of anti-Americanism out. So there are a lot of muted comments about adapting to a situation of power.

Yes, they know that the US has total superpower position in the weapons field. The US military budget today is as big as the rest of the world's military budgets put together. I think everybody will have to take that into account since they are demonstrating their military strength in the case of Iraq, even though the outcome might be nothing that they had wanted.

But, I can understand that governments are a bit cautious in their attitude. As to support on the streets, no. I think that the world is worried about the US throwing its weight around and I would also think that there is hope that the US government, the Bush administration, has learned something. No government is about to admit a mistake, especially not before an election and hardly even after the election. But I would hope that they are pragmatic and intelligent enough to see what did go wrong, because they must have seen that after all.

Q. If you look at history, you will see that sanctions don't work. If you take the threat of sanctions off the table what are the other alternatives that appear to be acceptable to your mind?

Hans Blix: The question about sanctions not working very well, is too generalised. After all, in the case of Libya the impression is that long years of sanctions did work and it was the main reason why Qaddafi wanted to get out of the straight jacket he was placed in and take the offer of carrots to be brought back into the fold.

In the case of Iraq, also, sanctions did work. From Saddam's interrogations we have learned that he has said that they wanted to get out of the sanction situation and, therefore, he said to the UN truthfully that they had done away with WMDs. That was true. But at the same time, he wanted to create an impression amongst his neighbours that maybe he was still dangerous. It was like hanging a 'Beware of dog' without having a dog. He miscalculated because he did not think that the US would go so far as to start a war.

Ajay Shukla (Foreign Correspondent, NDTV): When you think back with the benefit of hindsight, Dr Blix, do you believe now that you were just the fig leaf for a strategic plan of a far wider scope than just a handful of WMDs and if you could turn the clock back would you be far more unequivocal in giving Iraq a clean chit?

Hans Blix: When one talks about the US administration, I think one must be careful that it is the president who decides. There were, of course, people like Cheney and others who right from the beginning thought the inspection was ridiculous. Mr Cheney said the inspection is useless at best. So there wasn't much enthusiasm for going through with this procedure. I don't think Mr Bush, judging by what I have been reading by Woodward and others, had finally made up mind. Perhaps he was leaning towards an invasion. Maybe he was sceptical about inspections. We could see that even in February 2003, he asked me how long he could keep his options open.

Now, giving a clean chit is a more difficult problem. The Iraqis often said to us, 'Look if you bring someone before the court, the prosecutor has to prove that you are guilty or else you are acquitted. Therefore, we should be acquitted. You have not proved that we have any WMDs.' I explained that they were not like an accused in a criminal court. That they were in a certain situation where the world wanted them to act in such a manner that it was confident that Iraq did not have any WMDs. When people are acquitted from court due to a lack of evidence, it does not necessarily mean that they have won everyone's confidence.

So, the difficult task was to prove the negative. How can you prove the negative that there is nothing? That was the problem for the Iraqis and for us. I said in the Security Council that, yes, it is difficult. You cannot prove 100 per cent. I told the Iraqis you have to do better than this. So, in February 2003, they came to us with a long list of people they said had participated in the destruction of weapons in 1991. I think if the inspections had continued a few months longer we would have been able to go to all the sites, which British and American intelligence suspected, and report to the world that they did not have WMDs. We could have reported that though they were 100 per cent convinced that there were weapons, we had zero per cent knowledge of any. I think that would have made the war more difficult to start.

Regional Cooperation for

Growth and Prosperity

■

Dr Surakiart Sathirathai

■

K. Natwar Singh

■

Dr Surakiart Sathirathai

Minister for Foreign Affairs, Thailand

Surakiart Sathirathai is the youngest Finance Minister and now the youngest Foreign Minister of Thailand, not just in Thailand but in the Association of South East Asian Nations (ASEAN). Notwithstanding his age, he brings to his position a wealth of experience in international affairs, politics, academia and business.

On his return to Thailand, after earning a doctorate in law and international economics from Harvard University, US, Sathirathai, took up teaching at Chulalongkorn University and pioneered a programme of studies in international economic law. He was made Dean of the university.

Sathirathai's first political appointment was as Adviser and Head of Professional Staff Office of the House Foreign Affairs Committee in 1986. In 1988 he was made Policy Adviser to Prime Minister Chatichai Choonhavan and was involved in trade negotiations with the US on intellectual property rights. He is also given credit for his role in bringing a peaceful settlement to Cambodian issue.

As Finance Minister, he worked out a financial master plan for social development which lay the groundwork for the decentralisation of fiscal authority. In February 2001, Sathirathai was appointed Foreign Minister and has, since then, been responsible for carrying out a reorientation of foreign policy. During his tenure, Thailand has reinforced its ties with traditional allies and partners, as well as reached out to form new partnerships. To this end, he has been instrumental in bringing to fruition new foreign policy initiatives by Thailand, such as the Asia-wide Asia Co-operation Dialogue and Ayeyawady-Chao Phraya-Mekong Economic Co-operation Strategy, a sub-regional framework between Thailand and its mainland Southeast Asia neighbours.

Sathirathai has worked to address issues that confront not only developing countries but also the world: promotion of global free trade, combating international scourges such as HIV/AIDS and anti-personnel landmines.

FOR THOUSANDS OF YEARS THAILAND AND INDIA HAVE BEEN CONNECTED BY HISTORICAL AND CULTURAL TIES. IN LANGUAGE, FAITH, BELIEF, CUSTOM, TRADITIONS AND literature, we share historical roots. In trade, our merchants and tradesmen have fared prosperously over many centuries. In our way of life, so much of our Thai everyday life can be traced back to India. Bodh Gaya in the state of Bihar, where I had the chance to visit and pay my respects yesterday, is one of the most revered places that most Thai people would long to visit at least once in their lifetime. I had the honour of presenting His Majesty the King of Thailand's Kathina robe to the temple.

Our common heritage and cultural affinity continue to bind our peoples together and have created a sense of family amongst us. India is, and has always been, recognised as a cradle of Asian civilisation. In the past and in the present, we continue to value India's leading role in building a stronger Asia as well as her role in the multilateral system.

The *Hindustan Times* has done a great service in helping to reinforce and enhance the role of India and the world. This conference provides a platform for an intellectual debate on India's role in the world of the twenty-first century, where the strategic landscape has changed tremendously. India's role and contribution in the new strategic landscape will not only benefit herself, but also Asia and the rest of the world. This conference is also timely as we are preparing for the ASEAN[1]-India Summit in Vientiane Laos, another platform to consider India's role in Southeast Asia.

I wish to share with you India's importance in realising what would be the ultimate aspiration for all of us in Asia: our Asian community. I just cannot emphasise enough the leadership role that India has to play in the process of strengthening Asia-wide cooperation for mutual growth and prosperity. There can never be an overstatement on how India can complement and add value to cooperative endeavours for sustainable development and mutual

1 Association of Southeast Asian Nations.

prosperity in our region of Asia and the world at large. I would take the opportunity to examine how emerging networks and building blocks of subregional cooperation in Asia, including the linkages and bridges between them, can help forge a stronger sense of community within Asia and reinforce the foundations of multilateralism.

The debate on the opportunities and challenges of globalisation continues to be a recurring theme. Globalisation brings benefits to some and sufferings to others. Developing countries are grappling with the present-day realities arising from globalisation. To cope with globalisation is to learn to manage its impact. To manage its impact is to understand that globalisation is a human creation, human-made so it must be human-manageable for the benefit of all mankind.

We must look at all other parts of Asia, particularly another engine of growth, if our eyes are on the future

The borderless world of globalisation brings about the free flow of people, free flow of goods and services, free flow of financial funds and free flow of information technology. And as long as we benefit from them we seem to take them for granted, until we run ourselves into crises, as we did after the 1997 Asian financial crisis, the 9/11 tragedy, the scourge of epidemics such as SARS and Bird Flu, as well as the surge in oil prices. That's when we start to learn how to manage the dark side of globalisation.

We learn to seek a new paradigm of thinking on how to survive, how to grow, how to develop and how to sustain prosperity for the welfare of our peoples. In Asia, we learn not to fall victims of the dark side of globalisation anymore. We learn to turn our abundant resources, our differences and our diversity, our richness in population, reserves and savings into our strength, into harmony, into unity, into stability and into prosperity. And India today is well placed to create such strength, harmony, unity, stability and prosperity for Asia.

However, when we look at growth and prosperity in Asia, East and Southeast Asia loom large. The economic dynamism of Japan, the Republic of Korea and the emergence of China as the growth engines of Asia are more than apparent. In Southeast Asia, ASEAN is implementing its ASEAN Free Trade Arrangement or AFTA. ASEAN is expanding the free trade arrangements with several major trading partners such as Japan, China, Korea and India. ASEAN has even agreed to move towards the realisation of an ASEAN community comprising security, economic and socio-cultural pillars by the year 2020.

Beyond this, ASEAN is also working towards the East Asian community comprising the ten ASEAN members and China, Japan and the Republic of Korea. The movements towards an East Asian

South Asia, and encourage that region to become strength, harmony, unity, stability and prosperity of Asia.

community will have wide-ranging and long-term impact in Asia and beyond.

However, it cannot be right, and should not be right, to assume that Asia's growth engine is found only in East Asia. Indeed, we must look at all other parts of Asia particularly South Asia, and encourage that region to become another engine of growth, if our eyes are on the future strength, harmony, unity, stability and prosperity of Asia.

Here, in South Asia, the growth of South Asia is to encourage the progress of SAARC and I hardly need say that for SAARC to gain momentum and greater progress, India does play an indispensable role. India's recent role in revitalising SAARC and in holding dialogue with Pakistan has moved this South Asian grouping forward. The more rapid growth of South Asia and SAARC is both desirable and imperative for the people of South Asia, as much as for Asia as a whole.

Asia's strength should not depend on the lopsided prosperity balance. It may be a fact that for the time being East and Southeast Asia are growing faster than other parts of Asia but we must not let them run away with their economic growth and prosperity. Asia cannot afford to have its growth over-concentrated in one part of the continent, leaving others dragging so far behind if it is to realise its aspiration for an Asian community.

That is why Thailand recognises the importance of South Asia and its important role towards an Asian community. Thailand recognises the necessary linkages between South Asia and Southeast Asia in order to create inter-subregional partnerships. With Prime Minister Thaksin Shinawatra's 'prosper thy neighbour' and 'think beyond Thailand' approaches, we understand the need to bridge the developmental gap in a faster, more concrete and sustainable manner – not for the benefit of Thailand but for the benefit of all.

At home, we have been doing it with our adjacent neighbours of ASEAN. Thailand is bridging the developmental gap between the old and the new ASEAN members under a new initiative of economic cooperation strategy known as ACMECS[2] between Thailand and Myanmar, Laos, Cambodia and Vietnam. Initiated by Thailand last year, we hope that ACMECS will accelerate the narrowing of the developmental gap between the old ASEAN members and the new ASEAN members as well as leaving the latter with lasting and sustainable development.

And with South Asia we must create the bridge to narrow that gap between South Asia and Southeast Asia through the Bay of Bengal Initiative for Multi-Sectoral Technical and Economic Cooperation or BIMSTEC. The framework brings together Bangladesh, Bhutan, India, Nepal and Sri Lanka from South Asia on the one hand, and Thailand and Myanmar from Southeast Asia, on the other. Thailand hosted BIMSTEC's first ever summit in Bangkok in July 2004. The BIMSTEC leaders gave political impetus for the free trade arrangement among the seven countries, as well as adopted key cooperative projects initiated by India in security, tourism and energy cooperation. We hope that BIMSTEC will serve

2 Ayeyawady-Chao Phraya-Mekong Economic Co-operation Strategy.

effectively as another inter-subregional building block towards an Asian community. We look forward to the concretisation of the three key initiatives at the next BIMSTEC summit in India.

As for ASEAN and SAARC, the two organisations have established a formal link and cooperation mechanism for quite some time. But today, we need to see to it that the ASEAN-SAARC cooperation is for real and is given the necessary impetus. At the sixth ASEAN-SAARC meeting in New York, which I was honoured to co-chair with the foreign minister of Pakistan, we added a new dimension to our cooperation. We identified key areas of cooperation, namely HIV/AIDS prevention, transportation linkages, tourism cooperation and poverty alleviation, as well as the possibility of linking our respective free trade areas namely, AFTA and SAFTA.[3] I am convinced that ASEAN and SAARC have not reaped enough benefits of our complementary potentials and an ASEAN-SAARC Foreign Ministers' meeting some time in the near future would be a useful forum for the two regions of Asia to chart our road to growth and prosperity and the road that ultimately moves us towards an Asian community.

In both BIMSTEC and the ASEAN-SAARC frameworks, I am sure I need not reiterate the pivotal role of India in pushing forward these endeavours.

Let me now turn your attention to more cooperation frameworks in Asia.

In fostering Asia-wide growth and prosperity, India has a key role to play in engaging other sub-regional frameworks such as the Conference on Interaction and Confidence Building Measures in Asia, or what we call CICA. India's prominent role in CICA is evident. CICA aims at enhancing confidence from differences and at building a sense of security from diversity and at strengthening a culture of peace and tolerance. At the second CICA ministerial meeting in Kazakhstan, Thailand became the latest member and looks forward to working closely with India and the rest of CICA members.

3 South Asian Free Trade Agreement.

If we look to the west of our continent, the Gulf States Cooperation Council, or GCC, is also moving forward as a solid building block in west Asia. So if you ask what is happening in so far as regional cooperation is concerned in Asia, I would say, clearly, Asia is working on a number of regional and sub-regional arrangements. They can all serve as building blocks for multilateralism. But none of these building blocks truly has a continent-wide coverage, at least not until as recently as two-and-a-half years ago.

This leads me to turn to the ACD or the Asia Cooperation Dialogue which Thailand initiated in June 2002 as the first ever pan-Asian cooperation forum to generate partnership and strength of Asia from Asian diversity and differences. Here again, the role and contribution of India as well as major Asian players such as Japan, China, South Korea and ASEAN is indispensable. India has shown keen interest and active participation in the evolving process of the ACD from its inception. The ACD serves to fill in the missing links between existing intra-Asian cooperation arrangements. Now comprising twenty-six Asian members spanning the breadth and length of Asia, the ACD members represent members from ASEAN, SAARC, CICA, GCC as well as China, Japan and the Republic of Korea. The ACD aims to tap into the inherent strengths of Asian countries in order to yield mutual prosperity and sustainable development.

This framework represents a new paradigm of cooperation. The ACD takes the form of annual ministerial dialogues and joint projects in eighteen areas of functional cooperation ranging from key issues of tourism to SMEs (small and medium sized enterprises); energy security to agriculture; and ICT (information and communication technologies) to poverty alleviation. Participation in these projects is on a voluntary basis, and on each member's comfort level, readiness and comparative advantage. In this way, everyone has a sense of participation and willingness while no one feels isolated or left behind. Each of the eighteen projects has between ten to fifteen participants. But when put together, you get a cobweb of eighteen areas of cooperation with participation from all corners of Asia. This is how we, having recognised differences, build our strength based on diversity.

India's commitment to the ACD is significant in moving forward the ACD process. India plays an active role as a prime mover on biotechnology and transport linkages. Under the framework of the ACD, as agreed at the second ministerial meeting in 2003, Thailand is working closely with India in the financial cooperation project, particularly the development of an Asian bond market, which is the new financial architecture for Asia, initiated by my Prime Minister. The idea has gained increased region-wide support through the ACD process, and this has been concretised with the creation of an Asian bond fund last year. We expect a second fund of the ACD to be established in local denominated currency. India and Thailand's pledged contribution of US $ one billion to the fund, which is to be denominated in Asian currency, will open up an opportunity for the wealth of Asia to be invested in Asia for Asian development. As India emerges as a financial centre, we look forward to your role in helping to strengthen the Asian bond market.

As Asia seeks to reposition itself in the international strategic landscape where continent-wide cooperation has emerged in other continents, a call for an Asian community is by no means premature. What is happening in Asia today, intentionally or unintentionally, is the emergence of building blocks for a more effective multilateral system and a continent-wide cooperation.

Our house of Asian community is, albeit slowly, being built. Slow as it may, it needs to be built firmly on solid foundation and strong construction that is tailor made to meet the needs and requirements for Asian prosperity. Given India's wealth of resources, her unique achievement in building strength from diversity, her commitment to Asia and the role of India, past and present, in the making of Asia as I have described, India should stand out as one of the key pillars for building our Asian community.

Our house of Asian community can be built upon the roof of the ACD that has become our first continent-wide cooperation. Our house of Asian community should be founded on the four main pillars of China, India, Japan and ASEAN. Our house of Asian community must be built solidly by the four walls that consist of all the building blocks in Asia, namely, ASEAN plus three (China, Japan and the Republic of Korea), the East Asian Community, SAARC, BIMSTEC, CICA, GCC, for instance.

Indeed, the initiative for building an Asian community has been envisaged over half a century ago by the great statesman Jawaharlal Nehru at the Asian Relations Conference in 1947 where he articulated on the theme, *A United Asia for World Peace* and where he said: 'The time has come for us, peoples of Asia, to meet together, to hold together and to advance together.'

Fifty years on, we in Asia are forging partnership from diversity to lay a strong foundation for an Asian community. The vision of a new Asia is now in making.

As we look to the future and join hands with India to build a secure foundation for an Asian community, let us realise an Asian community that secures the blessings of peace and prosperity for all. Let us realise an Asian community guided by compassion and non-discriminatory principles. And let us realise that an Asian community must contribute to building an even stronger and more effective global system of multilateralism.

A new chapter of the history of Asia is being created today in every corner of our continent. Asia, with its richness and diversity, has for centuries been desired by the West. Asia, because of, as much as in spite of, its richness and diversity had been divided and deprived of the growth and development it deserved. Asia, abundant in its population, resources, culture and civilisation has never been given a proper chance to reap the benefits of its own potential.

But today, no more. Asia has learned its lessons in history. Asia has learned its lessons in globalisation. Asia has learned its lessons through its crises. Today, Asia has enough building blocks, pillars and roof to build a house of Asian community, a community for growth and prosperity for all Asia. Our task today is to reinforce and strengthen our building blocks, bridging the gap between them. Our task is to make sure that the pillars are strong enough to support the house. And our task is to make sure that the roof is big and wide enough to give coverage to the Asian community.

K. Natwar Singh

Minister of External Affairs of India

Natwar Singh has been India's External Affairs Minister in the Manmohan Singh cabinet ever since the government assumed office in May 2004.

A career diplomat, Singh joined the Indian Foreign Service in 1953 and served for thirty-one years. One of his earliest postings was to Beijing, following which he was transferred to New York, initially with the Permanent Mission of India, and subsequently as India's representative to the UNICEF executive board. Between 1963 and 1966, he served on several UN committees, until, in 1966, he was posted to Prime Minister Indira Gandhi's Secretariat.

Singh was part of the Indian delegation to the heads of Commonwealth meeting (CHOGM) in Kingston, Jamaica, 1975 as well as in 1979 when the meeting was held at Lusaka, Zambia. He was an Indian delegate to the 30th and 35th session of the United Nations General Assembly. From 1981 to 1986, he served as Executive Trustee, UN Institute for Training and Research.

In 1983, Singh was appointed Secretary-general of the Seventh Non-aligned Summit in New Delhi and was also Chief Coordinator of CHOGM held in New Delhi in the same year. In March 1982, he was appointed Secretary in the Ministry of External Affairs – a post he held until November 1984 when, after the assassination of Indira Gandhi, he decided to join political life.

Singh was elected to the eighth Lok Sabha in 1985 and was appointed by Rajiv Gandhi a Minister of State in the Department of Steel which came under the Ministry of Steel, Mines and Coal, and the Department of Fertilisers in the Ministry of Agriculture. In 1998, when the Congress Party came back to power, he was appointed Minister of State in the Ministry of External Affairs. In April 2002, he was elected to the Rajya Sabha.

Natwar Singh is highly regarded for his erudition and has published several books.

FOR THE PAST TWO DAYS YOU HAVE BEEN LISTENING TO VARIOUS LUMINARIES – THE PRIME MINISTER OF INDIA, SONIA GANDHI, JOHN MAJOR, HANS BLIX, THE FABULOUS Imran Khan – and you have heard it all. British Prime Minister Harold Macmillan while campaigning in 1959 was addressing a meeting in his constituency when a heckler at the back stood up and said to his wife, Lady Dorothy: 'You are sleeping. Why don't you listen to what your husband is saying?' And Lady Dorothy got up and said, 'My father is a politician, my husband is a politician, my son is a politician, my son-in-law is a politician. I have heard it all before and I am going to go back to sleep.'

So, you have heard it all, and if you would like to go to sleep, you are welcome.

It is exciting to be the foreign minister of a great country like India at this time. The nineteenth century was sold on the idea that progress is inherent in history. The twentieth century proved that this was not so: two World Wars and the invention of nuclear weapons are not signs of progress.

What is the legacy that the twentieth century has left to the twenty-first century? Beginnings have been rather bumpy in the past four years. But seven to eight years ago, I was invited to a symposium held in Seoul, organised by the government of Korea and the *International Herald Tribune* where one of the speakers was Mr. Alvin Toffler the great futurologist. He gave a brilliant presentation at the end of which I got up and said, 'Mr Toffler your vision of the twenty-first century is remarkable in technological terms, but you did not mention truth, compassion, love, sorrow, reason, wisdom even once. So as far as I am concerned, I would like to propose to this house, to adopt a resolution that, having heard from Toffler his vision of the twenty-first century, this house decides that the twenty-first century be postponed.' Now, since this is obviously not going to be possible, we have to see how best to deal with the opportunity and challenges of the new century.

This session is devoted to discussing regional cooperation, but I would like to place my remarks in the larger context of a rapidly transforming global order – and what India sees as its role in shaping the architecture of the emerging world order.

Our century is already beginning to look like a confused tangle of competing forces, confronting states with issues of governance for which there are few reference points, even in recent history. Our impulses remain rooted in our conception of nation states and yet there is virtually no challenge we are called upon to address, which does not have, at the same time, a regional or global dimension.

The line between what is the realm of domestic policy and what constitutes external affairs is constantly being eroded, demanding a degree of coordination and consultation within arms of government that are most comfortable working in compartmentalised hierarchies with clearly marked out territories. The challenge for India lies in its capacity to fashion a foreign policy that addresses concerns which have multiple dimensions and evolve an efficient instrument to deliver that policy. To borrow analogy from the military field, but with entirely peaceful intentions, not only do we need a potent warhead in the form of good policy, we also need an efficient delivery system in the shape of our external affairs establishment.

What is India's vision? What is the place we wish to occupy in the emerging international landscape? It should come as no surprise that as a flourishing democracy, India believes that democratic values are as relevant internationally as they are within our own country. Just as the rule of law is essential to democratic functioning within countries, so is it necessary to restrain the strong and safeguard the weak in the community of the nations?

Here we see a major role for the UN, which will be observing its sixtieth anniversary next year. What role does the UN play today in the international architecture? We believe it can play this role only after significant reform, reform that makes its structure and functioning much more democratic than it is currently. Most UN members today recognise the need for an enlarged and restructured Security Council with representation by more developing countries. India's claim to permanent membership arise not just because of our civilisational legacy or our representation of one sixth of humanity. They arise because we are the world's largest, most vibrant democracy and the fourth largest economy in terms of purchasing power. They arise because of India's unswerving commitment to the ideals and activities of the UN. They arise because of India's impressive record of participation in UN Peacekeeping Missions.

We also believe that a more democratic international order is also integrally linked to more equitable sharing of world resources, a recognition of our interdependence for sustainable development and the mobilisation of our considerable scientific and technological resources for the banishment of poverty from our midst. Development must return to the centre of our international discourse and we must endeavour to create collectively an economic environment where each nation and peoples have a credible opportunity to seek a decent livelihood with a sense of dignity and self-respect.

Just as we need an international political order that is based on law and accepted norms, so too, is there need for a rule-based multilateral trading system. We have to collectively acknowledge what has been increasingly evident for some time – islands of prosperity in a sea of poverty are simply unsustainable.

India wishes to play a leading role in shaping the global order that is in the making. We believe we can, and must, play this role not merely because we are a nation of a billion people or because we are an emerging economic powerhouse or because we have always been active in the international arena. We bring to the troubled and divided world our unique civilisational attributes. India is a multi-ethnic, multi-cultural and multi-religious society where plural democracy has been, despite a few setbacks, an outstanding success. Through the centuries, India has been at the crossroads of multiple influences and its creative genius has drawn strength from all the different cultures and religions that have found place in its welcoming fold.

For India, diversity is strength, not weakness. It is a source of creativity, not a threat to unity. At a time when the world is watching with anxiety the sharpening edge of assertive, ethnic and religious identifies, we are a living refutation of the pernicious theory of the clash of civilisations propounded by a professor at Harvard University in America. We believe that in resolving the contradictions that a globalising world is confronting, India is uniquely placed to deliver a message of harmony and creative coexistence.

This is how we have survived as a democracy for the last fifty-seven years. Our forte is crisis management; we are good at reconciling contradictions. If we were not good at crisis management or reconciling contradictions, our democracy would not function.

There is another reason why India is destined to play a leading role in the transformation that the world is undergoing. Classical economics made development the function of putting together land, labour and capital as the primary resources available to a country. Today, the critical resource for development is knowledge and the society of the future is the knowledge society. Countries which will be on the forefront of economic advancement and will lead change,

We need a more equitable international order, where decision-making, through the forging of broad consensus

instead of being overwhelmed by change, are those which have an abundance of human skills and command over knowledge, tempered by wisdom. In this perspective, India with its vast pool of skilled manpower, covering the entire spectrum of human endeavour, and not merely information technology, is well placed to make a significant contribution, by becoming a knowledge powerhouse for the entire world.

It is within this over-arching world vision and rooted in a unique civilisational ethos that we must conduct India's foreign policy. We have to recognise the ground realities that we face but we must also seek to transform them in line with our vision. No Government of India, whether Congress or non-Congress, has been able to alter that fundamental framework because we have not been able to come up with an alternative. If Jawaharlal Nehru was alive today, he would have responded to the changing international agenda and made suitable adjustments where they were necessary.

You will recollect that throughout the Freedom Movement, the Congress party was totally opposed to India having any link with the UK after we attained Independence – and this included our link with the Commonwealth. But when Nehru became Prime Minister he saw that he had to change his stance. He thought that the link with the Commonwealth was useful for India; it was in our national interest and so he made a fundamental change and made the Congress party accept that change.

Similarly, it does not make sense to me when it is said that non-alignment has become irrelevant. Non-alignment must be reinvented to make it relevant to the international agenda today: terrorism, HIV/AIDS, poverty, health, child infanticide. It is here that the Non-aligned Movement should come out with new ideas – and let's not confuse non-alignment with the Non-aligned Movement. The Non-aligned Movement needs diplomatic blood transfusion; non-alignment does not.

global challenges are addressed through collective and not through a process dominated by a few.

In international affairs what are the challenges that confront us today? To my mind, the world must adjust to the emergence of both China and India as major actors on the global scene. There is a clear sense that the two Asian giants have much to gain by cooperating together in nudging the world towards multi-polarity and multilateralism. And they are beginning to discover that each can contribute to the economic dynamism of the other as large developing economies. It is no accident that trade between us will probably exceed US $12 billion this year, and continue to grow at a breathtaking pace.

The world must also contend with the disappearance of the Soviet Union and its point of view. You may or may not have agreed with that point of view but at least it represented an alternative point of view. Today we have a multi-polar world, but we have one superpower and all nations of the world have had to adjust its relationship with the US – as we have done and are doing.

The disappearance of the Soviet Union has led to unprecedented global influence being exercised by just one country, as I said the US.

For us, relations with the US have a special place because we are both vibrant democracies. Our perspectives on specific issues may be different, and that may lead to differences in policies. However, we share a great and enduring affinity as peoples wedded to democratic values and today there is such a broad range of interaction between the two countries across the board, that the US election results do not fill us with any great uncertainty or doubt. Indo-US relations are beginning to acquire a degree of stability and predictability and a willingness to work together on shared concerns.

For India, Russia is a key interlocutor and a reliable partner. The challenge for both countries has been to manage the transition from the Soviet Union to Russia, even while the strategic convergences that underlay Indo-Soviet friendship continue to be valid. Today, there is need for India to engage with Russia at many different levels, interacting with many newly emergent constituencies in a much more diffused polity. This will be one of the major policy objectives of our government.

Another area of pre-eminent challenge for us is to create a congenial neighbourhood with peaceful and tranquil borders, and the pursuit of a common destiny of shared prosperity for the 1.5 billion people who inhabit our subcontinent. This has to be pursued in a complex environment, where the subcontinent is dominated in terms of area, population and economic resources by India and where India has land or maritime boundaries with all its South Asian neighbours. It is only natural, but not necessarily inevitable, that our smaller neighbours look upon India with some degree of apprehension. A key objective of our policy is to reassure our neighbours, and anchor this assurance in a virtuous web of cross-border, economic and commercial linkages.

Once India is looked upon as an opportunity, then its size and economic strength would become an asset rather than liability in dealing with our neighbours. The road to a South Asia, which is at peace with itself, lies in economic integration.

Yet another challenge that the world confronts is dealing with the menace of international terrorism. Terrorism threatens not only growth and prosperity but the very foundation of civilised democratic societies. This scourge respects no boundaries. The same bomb that kills and maims in Mumbai today can cause death and destruction in another part of the world tomorrow. For this reason, there can never be a category of 'good' terrorists and 'bad' terrorists.

The events following 11 September 2001, have created another challenge – how to deal with the problem of extremism and fundamentalism without wounding the self-respect of the Muslim world. Today, there are fifty-four Muslim countries which are members of the UN. There is no doubt that the unfortunate juxtaposition of terrorism and Islam has hurt Muslim psyche across the world from Mauritania to Medan. It is the responsibility of all of us to provide the healing touch. India with its history of interaction and coexistence with Islam for more than thousand years is again uniquely placed to assist in this process.

In pursuing all these objectives, the Ministry of External Affairs will coordinate policy with a number of other actors. At the central level, this involves working together with the ministries of home and defence, the economic ministries and security agencies. Equally important is regular consultation and coordination with the governments of bordering states. Currently, our effort is precisely to promote such consultation and coordination, making it a regular habit, rather than a sporadic event. In a very real sense we are witnessing a domestication of diplomacy which is changing the way we conduct our foreign policy.

Ours is a coalition government and it has been in office for less than six months. When it came to office, there were doubts expressed on whether it would have the capacity, or even the coherence, to deal with emerging challenges. These months have proved that we are equal to the challenge.

The first diplomatic crisis we faced was the hostage crisis in Iraq, and we came out successfully having saved the lives of our citizens without compromising our principles. With Pakistan, not only have we carried forward the dialogue process, we have also replaced a reactive mindset with a pro-active forward-looking strategy which is beginning to yield results. When Imran Khan said to me that he was very keen to visit Kashmir but was finding it difficult to get a visa I told him that a visa would be granted to him the moment he applies for it and that he is free to go to Kashmir for as long as he likes, meet whoever he wants to. We have no objection.

We did not let the change in government disturb the tempo of our engagement with the US and it is our government which was able to move decisively to conclude the Next Steps in Strategic Partnership or NSSP. It is this UPA[1] government which has brought India to the threshold of the United Nations Security Council permanent membership. We are working together with a large number of countries, including Brazil, Germany and Japan on the same platform and are grateful to the UK, France and Russia for supporting our claim for a permanent membership. Our ability to mobilise a majority of UN members in India's support was again on display when India won the highest number of votes in the recent elections to ECOSOC[2] – 174 as against 152 by even our neighbour China.

We have used all the tools of our diplomacy to support India's quest for reliable energy supplies, seeking and obtaining opportunities in Angola and Sudan in Africa, Kazakhstan in Central Asia and Myanmar in Southeast Asia.

We have made India an indispensable partner in every key region of the world. In two days from now, India and the EU will announce a strategic partnership, which will transform our relationship with an expanded union of twenty-five European countries. By any yardstick, this is a significant achievement for a government which has been in office for less than six months, and I can promise that there will be many more successes in the days to come.

1 United Progressive Alliance.
2 The Economic and Social Council.

Moderator | **Vir Sanghvi**

Eidtorial Director, Hindustan Times

Q. My question is to the Thai foreign minister. Sir, looking at you as the future secretary general of the United Nations, do you believe that the UN should be reformed or reconstituted? Do you believe in an enlarged Security Council?

Surakiart Sathirathai: I think it is time for the UN to be reformed, but not only the Security Council, but other organs as well. It is clear that the international political and economic strategic landscape of 1945 is totally different from what exists today. So, the UN would have to reflect the reality of today's international strategic landscape.

But we have to look at UN reforms comprehensively – not only in the Security Council. We should also look at the work of the General Assembly to streamline it to be more effective. We believe that we cannot have security without development and vice versa. But so far we don't have any particular organ of the UN that pays attention to development issues. We may have to look at the Trusteeship Council whose work is already complete to see the possibility of transforming it to an organ that can deal with the issue of development more effectively.

We have to look at the various means where we can strengthen the ECOSOC; we have to admit that the economic and social concerns of India and Thailand have been sidelined in the past. The trade issue is being handled by WTO. The major economic direction of the world is being handled by the G8, so the coordinating role in terms of setting the direction of major economic policies has to be strengthened in ECOSOC.

Now with regard to the Security Council as I said before, the security composition reflects the reality of 1945 not the present. We cannot have the Security Council handling security issues without realising the very important contribution of so many countries and India is certainly on the forefront of that example.

I don't think we can continue to maintain peace and security without realising the important role of India, Japan and perhaps several others, so I am all for the reform of the Security Council – not only the enlargement issue, but also on issues of greater transparency, the functioning of the Security Council and to see how other countries can work together to contribute to peace and security. How a country can be added to become a new member of the Security Council is something that we have to continue consulting each other on.

Vir Sanghvi: The question is addressed to Mr Natwar Singh. Many people are surprised by your time in office. I think it is not a secret, everyone here knows that when you became Foreign Minister many of us saw you as a sort of Rip Van Winkle: that you were a prisoner of a Cold War mindset, that you had not realised that the world had changed. People wondered how you would do as a Foreign Minister. But, in fact, as your speech shows, you have done very well as Foreign Minister. If there was ever a Cold War mindset, you seem to have come out of it.

What I want to know is this: did we caricature your views or did you come into office – you remember the baptism by fire when the press went for you week after week – realising the world had changed and so, moderated your stand?

Natwar Singh: Well, those of you who know me well should know that I am a reasonably well-informed person. I read books, even write for your newspaper, so I do not know where this preconceived idea that I was a fossil from the Ice Age came from.

If I took some time to get used to the idea that there are eight countries of what was Yugoslavia and that I did not know the names of their prime ministers – and that's not my fault because the prime ministers keep changing constantly – then it wasn't just me who was adjusting, but the whole world. The Soviet Union had disappeared and the world has still not fully come to terms with this reality. Those of us who joined the Foreign Service fifty years or more ago, our intellectual conditioning was that the Soviet Union used to support India in its fight against apartheid and colonialism and imperialism.

The international agenda has changed, changed drastically, and the twenty-first century has to cope with these problems. I was surprised that except for me no one else mentioned the fact even the very, very important issue of the world is how to deal with the Muslim world. This is a challenge which the most powerful country and the smallest country in the world faces. In our subcontinent alone there are 450 million Muslims out of the 1.3 billion in the world. Any foreign office, any foreign minister, must address himself to this problem.

So, yes the world has changed and one has to wake up to this reality. Maybe, I took a little longer. But these were preconceived and ungenerous notions with people sitting on judgment on a lot of issues about which they know even less than I do.

A state becomes successful only when it is truly able to accommodate the aspirations and the needs of its minorities.

India-Pakistan

Fast Tracking the Road

To Friendship

■

Altaf Hussain

■

Altaf Hussain

Founder, Muttahida Quami Movement, Pakistan

Altaf Hussain, founder and leader of the Muttahida Quami Movement (MQM), was born on 17 September 1953 in Karachi, Pakistan. One of eleven children, his father Nazeer Hussain and his mother Khurseet Begum migrated to Karachi from Agra in India at the time of Partition.

Keen to become a doctor, Hussain decided instead to join the National Cadet Scheme in order to defend his country in the aftermath of the 1965 India-Pakistan war. After a year's military training, he joined the Islamia College, Karachi, where he obtained a pre-medical degree.

It was during his university days that Hussain began to feel that a number of students were being deprived of admission in the pharmacy department where he himself was a student. He began to campaign against this discrimination. In 1979, he took admission in the Master's programme in pharmacy but was unable to complete the degree when a religious fundamentalist group evicted him from the university. However, Hussain continued his political struggle from the platform of the All Pakistan Mohajir Student Organisation.

This was a movement Hussain started for the rights of the voiceless minorities of Pakistan. It shook the foundation of the feudal system. In March 1984, Hussain decided to launch the Muttahida Quami Movement. By 1986, the MQM had organised more than five thousand rallies attended by hundreds of thousands of people throughout the Sindh province.

Under Hussain's leadership, the MQM has achieved a fair measure of electoral success. The MQM participated in the general elections of 1998 for the first time, managing to win 14 National Assembly and 27 Provincial Assembly seats, mainly in Sindh. It increased its vote bank in the general elections of 1993 and 1997.

Altaf Hussain currently lives in exile in London.

I WOULD, AT THE OUTSET, LIKE TO THANK THE INDIAN GOVERNMENT FOR GRANTING ME A VISA SO THAT I CAN SET FOOT ON THE LAND OF MY ANCESTORS. I THANK YOU very, very much.

I congratulate the *Hindustan Times* for the Leadership Initiative series of lectures. I sincerely hope it develops into a successful forum to further the search for global peace and prosperity. I am indeed honoured and privileged to be invited to share the stage with some of the most eminent leaders of my generation and to offer my humble views before such a distinguished audience.

This also happens to be my first address in the land of my forefathers and I am, therefore, mindful of the historical opportunity to try and place my views on partnership with this great country for a better world.

There are more than 190 countries in the world today. They all communicate with one another directly or indirectly. In this age of information technology it is not possible to conceal facts for any length of time. India has made giant strides in the field of IT and is recognised as the world's largest democracy.

Soon after Independence India got rid of the prevailing feudal system, thereby strengthening democratic institutions. The development of this democratic process not only kept the armed forces at bay but also boosted education among the masses. General education brought about a middle class, which has started to play a crucial role in politics and business. The democratic process in India proved to be the lynchpin for its industrial advancement, particularly in the field of IT. It is forecasted that in the coming fifteen to twenty years India will become one of the strongest economies of the world, if the rate of progress continues.

As soon as I stepped on to the soil of India, for the first time after fifty-seven years of Independence, and I felt the breeze, I felt it was mine. It was a sweet-smelling breeze, full of love and wherever I looked I felt I was amongst my own.

No one can tell who amongst us is a Hindu or who is a Muslim. We have the same genetic makeup; the same physique. The division of the subcontinent was the greatest blunder in the history of mankind. It was not a division of land but of blood, genetic makeup, culture, brotherhood, relations, hearts. We divided up relationships of blood. Who can say the division was right?

I am here before you because of the hospitality of the British government that has provided me with shelter because my own government, the government and establishment of Pakistan, does not allow me to remain alive in my own country. I have faced several assassination attempts; the establishment has used bombs and hand grenades to try and kill me. And my colleagues forced me, requested me, to leave Pakistan and go abroad and guide them from there.

I have now been in exile for the past twelve years. For the first time in twelve years I am stepping into the South Asia region. As I was flying from London to New Delhi, we flew over Lahore and I could see this on my TV screen. But I cannot visit the country.

I would like to take the liberty of briefing you about the emergence, philosophy and the political journey of the Muttahida Quami Movement (MQM). We are the third largest political party in Pakistan. We stand for equal rights and opportunities for all – irrespective of colour, creed, caste, sect, gender, ethnicity or religion. We strive tirelessly for tolerance, religious or otherwise, and oppose fanaticism, terrorism and violence in all their manifestations. MQM is committed to the introduction of an entrepreneurial free market economy, good governance and an independent judiciary capable of dispensing justice. We want transparent accountability, a free press and participation of women in all spheres of life.

Our immediate political objective is to change the corrupt medieval and feudal political system of Pakistan. We are, therefore, the only genuine party of the lower and middle classes, totally devoid of feudal lords or army generals. The support that we enjoy from the people of Pakistan has been amply demonstrated in the elections of 1988, 1990, 1993, 1997 and 2002. We started out in March 1984 as a *mohajir*[1] movement, out of the frustration of *mohajirs* in Sindh.

1 Term used to describe people in Pakistan who migrated from India during the Partition.

The Pakistani establishment tried to spread propaganda amongst Sindhi-speaking people from rural Sindh that we would end up usurping their rights. Today, our track record encourages even those Sindhi-speaking people to join us in large numbers.

Why then, you may well ask, are we a part of the government which perpetuates army rule by undermining democracy and its institutions?

We have paid a heavy price for pursuing our political objectives in a country where democracy is controlled. Given the circumstances which prevail, our desire to serve the helpless, deprived and exploited peoples of Pakistan have indeed led us into political arrangements which we are neither comfortable with nor would deem desirable under better circumstances. But the choice before us in Pakistan today is not President General Pervez Musharraf or democracy but between the army and even more army.

To place our politics in context, I would also like to briefly touch upon the loot and plunder of the wealth and resources of Sindh and Baluchistan, including the denial of their legitimate share from the federal revenues and, ever so increasingly, their due share of water the consequences in terms of the stark poverty in rural areas and the severe environmental damage seen in both provinces.

The scenario is so depressing that the leadership of the day openly admits that the country would fall apart if the army did not run its affairs. What does this tell you? To me it signifies a telling blow to the very idea of Pakistan, a homeland for the Muslims of the subcontinent, and the two-nation theory which continues to wreck untold miseries on the people of this region since the past five decades.

Muslims are fighting and killing each other on the basis of tribal and linguistic affinity. Sectarian strife is worse than ever before. Mosques and *madrassas*[2] are but flourishing businesses. The less educated the Pesh Imam, the more popular and affluent he is likely to be. The advocates of *Jehad*, a medieval concept to tame the infidel,

2 Religious school of Islamic learning.

are wantonly killing followers of the faith as they leave places of worship. Perhaps the idea of Pakistan was dead at its inception, when the majority of Muslims chose to stay back after the Partition, a truism reiterated in the creation of Bangladesh in 1971. If you need further evidence, look at the plight of three hundred thousand Pakistanis stranded in Bangladesh for three decades in their passage to the chosen land. They are unwanted by both Bangladesh and Pakistan; led by an unknown destiny.

The rights of the people who migrated to Pakistan from Muslim minority provinces of the subcontinent were usurped and they had to face high-handedness and injustice. We formed the MQM against these injustices. To crush our movement, baseless accusations were made against us and we were termed 'traitors' and targeted through state oppression.

In 1993, general elections were held during an army operation against the MQM. The army imposed a ban on the MQM from contesting elections from a few constituencies to allow the army's created group to win and to demonstrate to the world that the people of urban centres of Sindh did not support the MQM. In response to this illegal and unconstitutional ban, the MQM decided to boycott the general elections. On our appeal, the people of Sindh successfully boycotted the general elections that were witnessed by international observers.

As a result, the entire election process became dubious and high-ranking army officials had to request us to take part in the Provincial Assembly elections. With assurances of free and fair participation in the elections – with only a 48-hour notice – we participated and the people overwhelmingly bestowed their mandate in our favour. If the charges of terrorism levelled against the MQM had been true, the people of Sindh would have supported the army operation and would not have effectively boycotted the elections. Nor would they have given their mandate to the MQM. Despite this, the people's mandate was not respected and the state operation continued unabated against the MQM. We were not even allowed to peacefully protest against this operation within the country.

No one can prove that we have pleaded anybody else's case except our own at international fora, including the UN. We did, however, seek moral, political and diplomatic support from countries that stand for democracy and human rights. My representatives have met officials of the US and many European countries because we were pushed against the wall and forced by our own government to take our case worldwide.

And now, I revert to the topic of the seminar.

The title of the conference *India and the World: A Blueprint for Partnership and Growth* has a welcome, optimistic connotation. The themes of the future for the people of South Asia are indeed partnership and growth. Obviously, the first requirement for either to happen is that peace and normalcy must prevail. For much too long, Pakistan and India have been at odds. If we look around, we see unrest in Sri Lanka, Nepal and Bangladesh, Afghanistan is still looking for peace.

India and Pakistan, being the two largest countries in the region, need to demonstrate magnanimity and the necessary political wisdom and desire to truly seek peace. It should be possible to pursue a meaningful, sincere and composite dialogue with an open mind.

I wish to take this opportunity to place on record the sincere appreciation of the MQM of the recent initiatives by the successive prime ministers of India, President General Pervez Musharraf and all those who may have been involved in or contributed to the same. It is imperative that the current ambience be maintained to enable the process to evolve gradually. We see the approach in first tackling the issue of the creation of processes necessary for carrying on a dialogue as a wise one. It is quite clear that the necessary architecture is now slowly but surely falling in place in a manner which would impart continuity and stability to the dialogue process itself. It is also heartening that a wide-range of outstanding issues are being simultaneously addressed at several levels.

I would appeal in particular to our Kashmiri brothers and sisters to show, at this crucial juncture, the necessary sagacity to allow the Indo-Pak dialogue to proceed on the basis of mutual adjustment and agreement. It should be clear to all concerned that there can be no military solution to any of the contentious issues, let alone the issue of Kashmir. Neither for that matter can one resort to militancy and extremism. The mindless loss of lives, endless human rights violations and continuing depletion of developmental resources to deal with civil strife cannot be justified under any circumstances. As a representative of a persecuted minority forced to live in exile and to grieve the loss of colleagues and supporters through extra-judicial processes, I can well understand the agony of the Kashmiris.

Over seventeen-thousand *mohajirs* including leaders, supporters and their relatives have been killed during army and state operations. Thousands of *mohajir* families have been rendered destitute because their breadwinners have been extra-judicially executed, arbitrarily arrested or forced into hiding or exile. My 66-year-old brother Nasir Hussain and his 28-year-old son Arif Hussain were unlawfully arrested in the presence of their entire neighbourhood, brutally tortured for three days and, on 9 December 1995, extra-judicially executed. Both were non-political citizens of Pakistan.

The total number of casualties in the four wars, including Kargil, has been in excess of thirteen-thousand. Most estimates suggest that already more than fifty-thousand lives have been lost in Jammu and Kashmir alone – causing misery and grief to family members, distorting the normal pattern of life and virtually destroying the local economy. Who benefits from all this? Can the people of Pakistan and India afford it? Can they countenance the diversion of resources from their development programmes, health programmes and education?

Definitely not. Two million students are being taught currently in about fifty-thousand *madrassas* run by right-wing religious parties that are outside government supervision to promote a medieval ideology leading to the generation of fifteen to twenty-thousand new militants every year, year after year. Who will detoxify society? How will they be reintegrated into the mainstream? I pay tribute to Muslim leaders and intellectuals of India for maintaining moderation and not pushing Muslims towards fanaticism and *jehad*.

The confidence-building measures contemplated to bring the

peoples of both countries closer must be implemented vigorously. Let there be free people-to-people contact, let there also be cultural and social contact, sporting contact, political contact, economic contact, diplomatic contact and, if considered prudent by both countries, even military-to-military contact to further peace and harmony. Presently, 'people to people' ostensibly appears to be 'Punjab to Punjab' contact. But Sindh is also part of the region and therefore, her people deserve equally to freely interact with the people of adjoining states of India.

However, denial to reopen the Khokrapar Munabao border and ferry service between Karachi and Mumbai is nothing but stifling the rights of the people of Sindh. The people of Sindh are forced to take an expensive route via Islamabad to obtain visas and then to Lahore to catch a train or a bus. It is now incumbent on the governments of India and Pakistan to reopen the visa office in Karachi, which would further better the relationship.

I have recently aired a few thoughts on *Realism and Practicalism.* I will appreciate your comments on it. The spirit and essence of it is that we must accept the ground reality without blinkers. The reality today is that India and Pakistan are at loggerheads and, as a result, the region is in turmoil. Dialogue between India and Pakistan should be pursued and should not be held hostage to the Kashmir issue. Practicalism seeks ways for common or agreed grounds.

When we talk of Kashmir several procedural and allied issues crop up. Is it a bilateral issue? Do the people of Kashmir come into the equation? I have a habit of speaking freely without mincing my words. I intend continuing to do so and gladly invite my critics to correct me on the credibility and the plausibility of my views, objectively, in India, Pakistan and internationally. To deal with Kashmir, there has to be a basis or options on which the talks could take place.

What could those options be? Is the recently talked about 'Chenab Formula' an option? Is the 'Dixon Plan' an option? Could formalisation of the Line of Control (LoC) be an option? Are there any more options that we may not know about?

We also talk about UN resolutions but can they be enforced? If enforceable, why have they not been enforced in the past? What have the Tashkent and Shimla Agreements and the Lahore Declaration yielded? Practicalism and pragmatism call for acceptance of what is in existence or has been in existence, instead of arbitrary new ideas.

I understand that the people of Kashmir are also aspiring for independence. But even for this option, negotiation has to take place. Negotiation is the primary condition for all options. The LoC could well be used as the basis to begin negotiations by virtue of it being the ground reality which has existed for the past three decades. What I am saying is, use it as a basis or option to begin talks from until such time that a practicable alternative option is found. What is wrong with that? If both countries resolve that crossing this line would be considered aggression, doesn't it, in layman's terms, amount to an international border? If not, what is an international border?

And, if this is not an option, then what options are we left with? Another war? We have fought three wars over Kashmir; the governments may have achieved political victories and defeats, but what did the people achieve? Body-bags of soldiers and civilians, more widows and orphans, more taxes, contribution to war funds, poverty and backwardness. And, if we remain intransigent and squander this opportunity, the cost to be paid in the long term could be horrid.

Before I proceed further, I would like to quote from the Prayer of St Francis of Assisi (1181), 'Where there is hatred, let me sow love…' On the spirit of this prayer, I would like to request both India and Pakistan to stop sowing the seeds of hatred and start sowing the seeds of love.

My plea is to let good sense and logic prevail and to let our peoples prosper. Let us divert critically required funds from defence to the social and economic sectors. Our children need education; our villages need clean drinking water, electricity and medical care. Everywhere there is crying need for employment, better civic amenities and transport facilities. Let common sense prevail over arrogance and political expediency. Let us arm our children with education, health and hygiene rather than nuclear bombs and missiles.

I applaud President General Pervez Musharraf for making a bold and courageous statement that discarding plebiscite is an option. I have always maintained that it was never a practicable or implementable option. For the past fifty-seven years, the leaders of Pakistan have not only misled the nation but also failed them by keeping them illiterate, impoverished, hungry, thirsty and without health facilities under the rubric of Kashmir to benefit one province to the detriment of another.

The US, now the unipolar power of the world, and its Western allies have historically supported dictatorial and monarchical rulers in the developing world for their short-term gains and opposed the moderate, liberal and enlightened middle class as their sustained foreign policy. These policies and mindsets have always been election-centric. They failed to calculate the long-term repercussions of their foreign policies. These authoritarian and monarchical rulers deliberately promote religious, sectarian, ethno-linguistic fanaticisms on the strength of the unbridled support of the West to protract their rules. They have oppressed their people and produced Osama bin Laden, the Al-Qaeda and Saddam Hussein. And now to rein in these forces, the US and its allies had to wage a global war against terrorism in Afghanistan and Iraq. As a result of these wars, thousands of innocent people are being killed and millions are suffering for no fault of theirs but their rulers. Infliction of atrocities are resulting in psycho-reactionary actions amongst millions.

It is now essential for the US and its Western allies to review their policies. They should now support and nurture the moderate, enlightened and liberal middle class that is capable of dismantling the religious, sectarian and ethno-linguistic fanaticism and establishing democracies which would be mutually beneficial for their people and the West.

In the case of Pakistan, the historical and sustained support to the feudal-mullah-military alliance by the US and the West has already proved negative and has permeated rampant corruption, bad governance, denial of rights to the smaller provinces, illiteracy, impoverishment, unemployment and frustration amongst the general populace and above all religious, sectarian and ethno-linguistic fanaticism and violence.

South Asian countries, in general, and India and Pakistan, in particular, need to do no more than draw lessons from Europe whose post-war history is roughly the same length as our two nations. The European Union which emerged out of the dictates of the economic well being of its people and the desire to fully actualise their individual potential in a collective manner, is a live demonstration of the possibilities that can be envisaged by the dynamic minds of visionary leaders. We should yearn for the day when we have a common union, perhaps even a common currency, while maintaining our sovereignties and dignities intact.

We have SAARC more in form than in content due to the rancour which has blinded us. South Asia remains one of the most unintegrated regions of the world. We are looking forward to the implementation of SAFTA (South Asia Free Trade Agreement) in January 2006 as outlined in the SAARC declaration of January 2004 in Islamabad. The creation of a free trade zone along with some degree of economic integration of SAARC countries could turn the region into a huge regional economic market, second only to China in terms of size. If futuristically developed, along with a network of roads and railway connections to Southeast Asia and Central Asia, the future of our succeeding generations would indeed be bright.

Restrictions on bilateral trade have forced both countries to import goods from third countries, while they could have been traded far more economically and efficiently from each other. Indo-Pak trade would ensure cheaper raw material, low transportation and lower insurance costs, resulting in the potential for quality products at competitive prices for consumers in both countries and larger markets for manufacturers.

Having resolved the external issues, South Asian countries need to put their houses in order. They should stop discrimination on the basis of ethnicity, religion or descent. I request the government of Pakistan to recognise and indemnify all religious and ethno-linguistic and national minorities and treat them equally to foster a sense of ethno-linguistic pluralism and nationalism. All governments in the past have deliberately strengthened ethno-linguistic particularism in Pakistan under the rubric of numerical majority and power. In democracy, only numbers should not count. A state becomes successful only when it is truly able to accommodate the aspirations and the needs of its minorities. Pakistan should genuinely strive to devolve power to the provinces making them fully autonomous, reserving for the federal administration only defence, foreign affairs and currency.

If the federation of the United States of America can remain strong by having fully autonomous states then why should one assume that a federation of Pakistan would weaken if the provinces have fully autonomous status?

Mainstream political forces, including the MQM, equipped with liberal and progressive ideological underpinnings have the capability of transforming Pakistan into a democratic and progressive state at peace with itself and its neighbours. They can deliver good governance, an independent judiciary and freedom of the media.

The purpose of this conference is to discuss and prepare a road map for the economic, strategic and political future of India in relation to the world and regional countries. To attain this objective we should find out the key to achieve positive results which is peace in the South Asia region. The region is the first gate to be opened and then we should proceed to open the second gate, which is the world.

The word peace is a catalyst to positivism, success, prosperity, harmony, better economy, better understanding and relations with neighbours.

If regional countries have peace and better relations it would ultimately draw the remaining world towards the region. Peace is the only key through which India can have improved and long-lasting relations with the world. But this peace must be established in the region first. The benefits that could be drawn by South Asian countries, including Pakistan, through peace can never be achieved through the use of nuclear weapons, atom bombs, chemical and biological weapons or a massive army.

India and Pakistan have considered each other enemies since Independence but now to achieve the sacred objective of peace, better and long-lasting relations, both countries will have to engage in a meaningful and sincere dialogue and cease all hostilities against each other.

Finally, I think South Asia needs to have a comprehensive human rights code that protects its peoples from unbridled state power. Freedom from poverty, hunger, illiteracy and the provision of basic services to be a part of human rights.

I am sorry if I have not been able to control my sentiments in this land because I still feel this is my home. You are my people and I am yours.

Moderator | **Karan Thapar**

Television Anchor

Sanjay Singh (Tata Group): Do you see the political boundary between Pakistan and India ever dissolving like East Germany and West Germany?

Altaf Hussain: We have reached a dead end where we cannot move ahead. The only option is to reverse to a respectable relationship of friendship, free trade and the opening up of routes. I hope the day will come when we can share the same position as that of European countries where people can visit each other without a visa.

Q. You spoke of making the LoC an international border. Why not just freeze this Kashmir problem for twenty years, let India and Pakistan make good relations?

Altaf Hussain: I am sorry I have already spoken on this matter. I have said please consider LoC not as a permanent border, but at least a point to start from. I want to add that the plight of Kashmiris can be resolved better by the Kashmiris. If they want independence, then I would go with them on it.

'If I had to predict what the Bush Administration will do in its second term, it will be precisely to try to bring about a big step towards an international order that most relevant societies feel they can embrace.'

India's Role

In the Changing World

■

Dr Henry Kissinger

■

Dr Henry Kissinger

Former Secretary of State, United States of America

Henry Kissinger has held almost every conceivable foreign policy position in the US government. Arguably, he is one of the most brilliant minds ever placed at the service of American foreign policy, as well as one of the shrewdest, best-informed, and most articulate figures ever to occupy a position of power in Washington.

Kissinger has been both National Security Advisor and Secretary of State, a Harvard academic and US army captain, a Nobel Peace Prize-winner and Chairman of a private consulting firm, Kissinger Associates. His most recent accomplishment was to chair an investigation into the 9/11 attacks at the behest of the White House.

During his years at the helm of US foreign policy, Kissinger steered his country through a complex international situation. Two of his major geopolitical accomplishments were to engineer the US withdrawal from the Vietnam War, for which he shared the Nobel Peace Prize in 1973, and to completely turn around the US relationship with Maoist China. Kissinger has also received the Presidential Medal of Freedom and the Medal of Liberty. He was also a tireless shuttle diplomat for peace in West Asia and nuclear arms control between the US and the Soviet Union.

The Germany-born Kissinger has written at length about the difficulties of being a representative of a liberal democracy practicing foreign policy in a world of hard-nosed power politics.

The aim of Kissinger's foreign policy has always been world stability and peace. And, as revealed in the voluminous memoirs of his years as the world's statesman among statesmen.

Drawing on his past experiences with some of the most important foreign policy leaders of our time, as well as his current experience as an international corporate consultant, Kissinger advances our understanding of international relations and the resulting impact on our domestic economy and security.

IT IS ALWAYS AN EXCITING EXPERIENCE FOR ME TO VISIT INDIA. IT GIVES ME AN OPPORTUNITY TO RENEW FRIENDSHIPS THAT HAVE DEVELOPED NOW OVER DECADES. This is a particularly important moment when, I believe in both countries, it is recognised that the interest of India and of the United States are parallel, and we have been able to develop a partnership that will be of great significance to the rest of the world.

Before I go into this, however, I need to point out that I speak here as a private citizen, a close friend of the administration and of its leading personalities, but I give my interpretation, which I believe is compatible with their general direction.

I speak to you as somebody who has thought a great deal about American foreign policy and history for quite a bit. But what I say is bound to be in the context of existing states and existing American relationships. We attach great importance to our relationship with India. But it is only fair to point out that we also have other relationships and that these must be understood in the context of their own history and their importance. In our view, they need not detract from the relationship we have with India.

We have just had an election in the US. If you had been in New York during that election, you would have thought that Senator John Kerry would carry forty-nine states. What the election has proved is that there is substantial national support for the fundamental philosophy that President George W. Bush represents – and that philosophy will be increasingly bipartisan as time goes on.

Foreign policy should not be considered the policy of one party. Foreign policy affects the fundamental interest of our society and has to be conducted over several administrations over an extended period of time. This is true of the relationship to India.

We in the world face four major problems. The first is one, which we called terrorism. The second is proliferation. The third is the movement of the centre of gravity from the Atlantic region to Asia. And the fourth is the impact of a globalised economy on the world economic system. This change brings about a dramatic transformation of international relations. I will conclude with expressing my conviction of the overwhelming majority of those who are concerned with foreign policy in the US, that the US and India can walk a parallel path. Indeed, we are two great nations that have no conflicting national interests that could bring us into confrontation – and that should be a fundamental theme for our foreign policies.

First, the issue is terrorism. In order to understand its impact on the US, you have to recognise the peculiarities of American history. America is the only major country in the world that has never had powerful neighbours. It is the only major country that believes that it could withdraw or participate in foreign policy at its own choice. It is the only major country that for most of its history has believed that every problem had a solution and that, therefore, once you faced a problem you could overcome it and set a deadline for it. If you look at American initiatives in the period after World War II, you will see that almost every one of them had a terminal line attached. Now, we are in a world in which there is no endgame, a world of huge revolutions going on in many parts simultaneously.

The fact that the US could be attacked on its own soil was a dramatic event for Americans, something that in India would not be in itself unusual in terms of Indian history. Secondly, this attack took place by private groups, not states. The whole of American history has been concentrated on international relations as the relationship of states to each other. This is true also of the European approach to foreign policy. That private groups could undertake efforts that in the past would be possible only by states – and that security was endangered by groups that had no attribute of sovereignty but were operating from the territory of sovereign states without identical motives was a novel departure. It forced the US to consider policies that were unprecedented and for which there is no preparation in our experience.

We had been familiar with diplomacy and deterrence in the Cold War. But deterrence does not operate against groups that have nothing to defend. And diplomacy does not operate with respect to groups that have no stated objectives and that are not willing to limit their objectives.

What we confronted, and what the whole world confronts, is not terrorism as such. Terrorism is a method. It is not a strategy. It is not a policy. We are facing radical, fundamentalist Islam that is trying to undermine secular Islam, moderate Islam secular states everywhere, and all other institutions that are incompatible with their radical vision of some sort of Islamic Caliphate. That is what the US had tried to oppose and that is what makes the policies that we had to pursue not just policies for the US, but policies that affect the whole world.

I will not go into the details of the diplomacy that led to Iraq. Nor do I accept the statements that I have heard. In the view of the US' leaders, this was not an issue of unilateralism against multilateralism.

Let me make clear what I believe to be the issue on unilateralism versus multilateralism.

We are at the beginning of a new international order. A new international order can last only if most of the significant nations believe in it. No nation, not even a nation as powerful as the US, can impose a world order on everybody else. Hegemony cannot be the permanent policy of a country. No empire has ever lasted because when running an empire is beyond the capacity of any society, it exhausts society in acts of repression.

So, the ultimate goal of America is to achieve some degree of consensus. And if I had to predict what the Bush administration will do in its second term, it will be precisely to try to bring about a big step towards an international order that most relevant societies feel they can embrace – which is one reason why the cooperation of another great democracy like India is essential.

The issue of unilateralism against multilateralism arises, or should arise, basically only in emergency situations – when a country feels that its vital national interests are threatened and it cannot achieve consensus. Then it has to decide whether to act alone or whether to give other nations a veto over something it considers essential for its security and survival.

That was the issue as it presented itself on Iraq: a country that had the largest armed forces in the region, that had used its armed forces to attack two of its neighbours, that had larger resources which it could deploy in that situation and that was believed to be in possession of, and working on, weapons of mass destruction could not be allowed to join the terrorists, especially as it had committed seventeen violations of the UN certified ceasefire that ended the Gulf War. I don't want to repeat the debates, but these were not trivial decisions nor are they a necessary guide for the future. The guide for the future should be to see what we could learn from this experience and how, before there is an emergency, we can achieve cooperation among the key countries relevant and international order.

Let me illustrate this with the current situation in Iraq. Whatever you think of how the situation arose and, as I made clear, I supported the policy of our administration, I would be amazed if many thoughtful Indians would not agree with me when I say that if a Taliban-type or fundamentalist radical government emerges in Baghdad it would radicalise the entire Islamic world and create fundamental challenges to moderate and even secular regimes in the Islamic world and to any country that has large Islamic minorities.

From that point of view, the outcome in Iraq is of great consequence to many nations. We have seen terrorism from Bali to Indonesia to Singapore to Turkey to Riyadh to Morocco to Madrid to Moscow. This is a world problem and when we ask ourselves how we should proceed in Iraq, my view – which is not yet, and may never be, the US government view – is we had to act unilaterally in the military field but we should seek multilateral support for the political institutions.

Once elections are held in Iraq, the evolution of Iraq would benefit from the cooperation and wisdom of other countries that have much at stake. It would be helpful, and I have said so publicly, if some kind of contact groups were created in which I have taken the liberty of mentioning India, and also Russia, Turkey and whatever European and Arab nations choose to cooperate, particularly those who have had experience with radical Islam. Political and economic reconstruction done cooperatively would separate the issue of military participation from the issue of political evolution. Such a cooperative effort which should also be a significant effort to bring about progress towards the Palestinian issue.

The second issue I mentioned is proliferation. This again is one that affects everybody. Indeed it is the sort of issue with respect to which, the US is in a better technical position against specific dangers like long-range missiles. The danger of the spread of nuclear weapons technology to other countries and into terrorist hands can best be analysed if we ask ourselves this question: what should be the reaction if there were a nuclear attack in any capital of the world from New Delhi to any European or American city? What would we do if that happened? At what point would we decide, and by 'we' I mean the international community, that it cannot go any further and we must insist on a solution, even an imperfect solution?

How much time do we really have and what countries are we most concerned about? At what point will the diplomacy of non-proliferation run out of control? This is a technical question and our scientists should be able to give precise answers. It is not helpful to come up with little measures and to have analyst discussions of whether pressure or diplomacy is better when the key issues remain unresolved.

The second question we have to answer is what precisely must one be to prevent real catastrophe from happening? What would one propose if there were a reasonable diplomacy that is in the decent interval including the proliferating country? Finally what do we do if diplomacy fails? I am not here to give you the answer to this, but I think these are key questions and I would not be surprised if the US raises them.

In building an international order it is not enough to insist on a diplomatic multilateral process but it is also not enough to insist on your own conclusions on every problem. I am convinced that in the first term President Bush had to deal with an emergency and this became the focal point of many frustrations. In the second term he will want to leave a historic legacy and I think he is in a position, comparable to one which the US was at the end of World War II, that is to say the period between 1945 and 1955 which witnessed some of the most constructive American diplomatic initialives.

The US contributed through the Marshall plan[1] and through many other measures to create and support an international system that managed to get us through the Cold War without catastrophe and managed to bring democracy to many countries. This is our challenge now. It is a particular challenge because as Prime Minister Manmohan Singh has pointed out, the centre of the gravity of the world is moving from the Atlantic to the Pacific to Asia.

The major productive capacities are gradually moving to Asia. The rate of growth in Asia is extraordinary and therefore a new international system will emerge. When you read European history you will find that it is generally argued that the emergence of Germany unbalanced the European system because it was too powerful a state for the environment and that it inevitably led to World War I. In fact, the British Prime Minister Disraeli in 1871 when Germany was unified said, 'This is a greater event than the French Revolution.'

Now we see the emergence of China; a little bit behind it is the emergence of India. This represents a greater transfer of power than any we have seen in a previous period and the relations of these countries to each other and to their neighbours will shape many of

1 On 5 June 1947, Secretary of State George C. Marshall spoke at Harvard University and outlined what would become known as the Marshall Plan. Europe, still devastated by the war, had just survived one of the worst winters on record. The nations of Europe had nothing to sell for hard currency, and the democratic socialist governments in most countries were unwilling to adopt the draconian proposals for recovery advocated by old-line classical economists. Something had to be done, both for humanitarian reasons and also to stop the potential spread of communism westward. The US offered up to $20 billion for relief, but only if the European nations could get together and draw up a rational plan on how they would use the aid. For the first time, they would have to act as a single economic unit; they would have to cooperate with each other. Marshall also offered aid to the Soviet Union and its allies in eastern Europe, but Stalin denounced the programme as a trick and refused to participate.

the significant events – indeed in a historical perspective it may be more significant than even our immediate concern with terrorism.

When I come to India, I am asked this question: are you going to try to play China against India or India against China and are you going to do a sort of balance of power policy in Asia? My answer to that is here we are dealing with two great nations with a long history. They are not toys with which the US can do what it wants. We cannot go to nations and say, 'Will you kindly conduct an anti-India policy because that is convenient for us,' or, vice versa, go to India and say, 'Will you help us balance China?' Both countries will act in their own perceptions of their interests. For America the key goal will be – or should be – to develop policies compatible with both.

In the period before World War I, that was a reasonable way to think, largely in terms of the balance of power though the catastrophic casualties of that war showed the danger of exclusive reliance on equilibrium. In the period of nuclear weapons and global growth, a war between major countries is a catastrophe; every leading state knows it will destroy the societies that engage in it. Which European statesman on 1 August 1914 – when the First World War broke out – would not have recoiled had we known what the world would look like in 1918 when the war ended?

We know today what the world will look like after a great power conflict. So the issue is not what balance of power game the US or India or China is going to play. I think the objectives must be much more profound.

I said globalisation is the key issue and it is the key issue in at least four ways. First, amongst industrialising nations, as one looks at the future, the access to energy and raw materials will become an increasing challenge and we may find the ironic result that some nineteenth century problems repeat themselves in a different way. A book called *The Great Game*[2] described the impact of Russia and Great Britain and, to a lesser degree, China on each other in Central Asia during the nineteenth century. It was about territory and Russia

2 *The Great Game: The Struggle for Empire in Central Asia* by Peter Hopkirk.

approaching the borders of India and of England wanting to protect its access to India.

I always point out to American audiences about Indian foreign policy and enterprise, the foreign policy of Britain, East of Suez was not made in London but in Kolkata, so that it reflected the Indian perception of fundamental Indian interests. It would be ironic if 'the great game' repeated itself about which way pipelines are going, whether east or west or south. It does not take any great imagination to know that if you leave it entirely to market forces without some strategic understanding, huge consequences could follow.

Then we have within and between nations, the challenges of globalisation, and the impact of globalisation. The American elections witnessed a debate about outsourcing and the danger of competition from China and India. The reason for that is obvious. Free markets help everybody in the long run. But in the short run, competition creates disparities and there is always a great temptation to use the political process to protect yourself against its economic consequences. Leaders have to understand this and, therefore, the G7 and G8 processes have to be used in a more profound and systematic way. When the G7 process was created in 1975 only three leaders sat at the table: the Prime Minster (or Chief Executive), the Finance Minster and the Foreign Minister. Therefore, the meetings were very small. Now they have become performances in which subordinates prepare the communique's and the meetings themselves become simply symbolic representations.

Now there is the challenge of globalisation between nations. Prime Minister John Major pointed out the inequalities that exist in the world and that you cannot have an international system in which most nations do not feel a sense of participation.

I have sketched for you some of the challenges the world faces. Now where do India and the US fit in this? For one thing, we are both democracies and this creates a certain proclivity in feeling more comfortable with regimes and governments that we know reflect the popular world and therefore assure greater continuity.

Secondly, we have no conflicting interests in the traditional sense.

That does not mean we cannot occasionally get on each other's nerves – we have proved a great capacity for that and I have made my own contribution to it – but when we look at our fundamental interests; at what we really want and what are we trying to achieve in the world, our disputes should be more than tactical disagreements. In the fundamental drift, our two countries can work closely and increasingly together.

The national purpose is no longer to create a balance of power because with modern weapons you don't have to add countries to achieve great power. The purpose is to deal with the intangible and economically tangible consequences of a globalising world, which is simultaneously in turmoil on many political issues. I expect that in the second Bush term, the relation between our two countries will grow even closer and that we can both learn from each other.

I expect that our countries will have a closer relationship without detriment to other relationships that we may have. That is our challenge. Over two hundred years ago, the German philosopher Kant[3] wrote: 'Someday there will be perpetual peace and it will come about either by human insight and human foresight or it will come about by a series of catastrophes of such nature that mankind has no choice.'

Our challenge in the world today is to make perpetual peace come about through human foresight and I expect that America and India will be partners in that effort.

3 Immanuel Kant (1724-1804).

Moderator | **Lalit Mansingh**

Former Indian Ambassador to the US

Q. Dr Kissinger, twenty-five years ago you wrote in the *White House Years* that America finds it easy to deal with dictatorships and finds it difficult to deal with democracies because the decision-making takes that much longer. It is nice to know that you see a great friendship growing between India and the US, but at the same time the US is also friendly with Pakistan where a dictatorship exists. Do you see any contradiction in your observation?

Henry Kissinger: Well, *White House Years* has about 1400 pages and while my students are required to memorise every word, I don't believe I said this because that is not my view. What I certainly believed in 1971 given the circumstances that then existed – in which India had made an agreement with the Soviet Union and we had opened to China but before Nixon's visit – there was a war that threatened the existence of Pakistan and so, for strategic reasons, we tried to bring this to an end.

The issue had nothing to do with the emergence of Bangladesh. I think the real issue was that India did not want Bangladesh to emerge as an American project. I can understand very well being the neighbour, but that was a purely strategic decision for a limited period of time. Institutionally, we always felt more comfortable with the Indian system than with the Pakistani system of military dictatorship which then existed and which was a military dictatorship.

It can happen that in the evolution of a policy, you encounter relationships that you believe are essential for your security in which you modify some of your other preferences. I am sure there are Indian officials here who remember very well what I said to them privately, that is, I always believed that the strategic interest of the US and India were largely parallel.

But in the Cold War, when Russia was 400 miles away for you and thousands of miles away for us there were different perspectives. That is not the case today and also the significance of domestic institutions is better understood today than it may have been at the height of the Cold War.

Chinmoy Gharekhan (Former Indian Ambassador to the US): Two brief questions. Since you are so close to the Bush administration it would be of interest to us to know your views on permanent membership for India at the Security Council. Second, what is your assessment of the post Arafat situation in the Middle East?

Henry Kissinger: To answer your second question first. I believe we are not at a point where significant progress can be made. I know this sounds ludicrous in the light of the circumstances that exist but the challenge of the Palestinian issue was that there was one point of view that said, 'Go back to the 1967 border, give up all the settlements and there will be some sort of guarantee.'

But there is no guarantee that can really work in that situation. Now that the security fence is being built, if it can be brought into some relationship to the 1967 border and if in return Israel does what emerged as a possibility in Camp David – that is, give up some of its current territory even if it is largely symbolic – we could see an agreement that brings together the concerns of Arab dignity and Israeli security.

It requires, however, that Europe and the US and other friendly countries come up with a common position to avoid the impression that America is the spokesperson for one side. If this unity could be achieved, I could imagine that even some moderate Arab countries could assume some responsibility for the difficult decisions that Palestine leaders have to make. Now, this a sketch but I am hopeful that America will try to take a lead towards this.

The death of Arafat makes it perhaps somewhat easier from some points of view and a little more difficult from other points of view because there is no central dominant authority left. What is important is that those who really want peace, stop competing with each other about who could appeal best to which of the two sides and achieve a common position that they will then sustain. If that is achieved, then I believe significant progress could be made within the next year to eighteen months.

Regarding India's membership to the Security Council. The present Security Council does not reflect the actual distribution of power in the world. It makes no sense to have India, Japan, Germany and, potentially, Brazil excluded from the Security Council. So, a discussion of the subject is extremely important. The problem, however, will arise with how you distribute that power. If you have, say, nine permanent members the veto would make no sense. Or if, say, Europe gets one vote rather than several, you get into transformations that affect the domestic politics of many countries. Realistically the US will not give up the veto. It is impossible in the American political situation to imagine that any President could even propose it, and inconceivable that any Senate would ever give it two-thirds majority.

What one could imagine, for example, is that we have new members who are permanent but don't have a veto. But, it does not make any sense to have India outside the Security Council and Japan and China in it and so this is a discussion that must be started in which I am favourable to having a Security Council that reflects the actual distribution of economic and political power. But I don't know exactly how to do it.

L.M. Singhvi (Former Indian High Commissioner to the UK): We expect a prescription for the second Bush administration, a prescription for the government headed by Dr Manmohan Singh and a prescription, which is meant for the people of both the countries. We would also like to know whether you think that America would continue to be constrained and conditioned by their other relationship, in this case their relationship with Pakistan, in respect to dealing with India.

Henry Kissinger: With respect to the first question, I say and I believe that will happen over the next years. An intense consultation with India in many fields on the government level, not so much with dealing with actual problems in our relationships – although that too should happen – but an intense discussion of how we visualise a potentially common future. How do we look at what I described about the energy problem, for example? How do we view the scientific evolution that will affect human life and the problem of development, and I think we should do that with an, at least, five year perspective, side by side with whatever current issue.

How does it affect our relationship with Pakistan? We have friendly relations with Pakistan – and I know that is an extremely sensitive point for India. We have no conceivable interest in promoting conflict between Pakistan and India. We would welcome greatly a reconciliation between India and Pakistan. Pakistan is a significant regional country. India is a global country, so those relationships have to be seen in that perspective and if we elaborate our relationships on that basis, it will automatically answer a lot of these questions.

We have absolutely no interest in building on the Indian subcontinent a kind of European balance of power situation. Of course we believe in the territorial integrity of every country but our fundamental concerns are different and that is the basis for a relationship in which the distinction will emerge quite clearly provided we really go to work, as I know our administration wants to. It is my impression from what the Prime Minister said here and what I got from my conversation with him.

Vinod Mehta (Editor, Outlook): My question to you is that since American society domestically is so vertically and visibly divided about the Iraq war and Senator Kerry's entire campaign was based on this, how will President Bush pursue a different policy in the face of this opposition?

Henry Kissinger: Well, if democratic elections mean anything, Senator Kerry lost the election. But I don't want to press on this because President Bush has pointed out that he wants to govern with the approval of at least a large segment of the Kerry voters. Now, as I told you, I supported President Bush's decision for strategic reasons because I thought it was too dangerous to leave this situation as it is and at the same time move forward on the war against terrorism. It is pointless to discuss and repeat the debates of two years ago, but if a Taliban type regime emerges in Baghdad or if Iraq becomes a centre of civil wars in the Arab world, this would be a disaster for every country.

So, the important question now: do I think the US will act unilaterally in every situation? In my view, the US will make every effort to achieve consensus but the best way to do that is before a crises arises. The second question is where do we go from here? The best outcome for America and for everybody else is the emergence of a government in Iraq that can govern with the support of its people and the support of an overwhelming majority of the world.

Having said this, that is huge task and you can't just snap your fingers and bring it about nor do I think can we do it alone and this is why I am now speaking strictly alone. This is not an official position. Some sort of contact group should be created of countries that have an interest – without asking them to participate in a military effort but to participate in a political and economic effort.

It is irrelevant whether the war was unnecessary as Senator Kerry claimed. I disagreed with him but we don't have insist on that point today and you may have noticed that Senator Kerry in his very generous and far sighted concession statement specifically mentioned the important of bringing Iraq to a successful conclusion. On this Americans should unite and I hope that we can have discussions with India and other nations to work on a cooperative solution.